HARDPRESS.NET
HOME OF HARD-TO-FIND BOOKS

The Strange Adventures of Captain Dangerous
by George Augustus Sala

Address:
HardPress
8345 NW 66TH ST #2561
MIAMI FL 33166-2626
USA
Email: info@hardpress.net

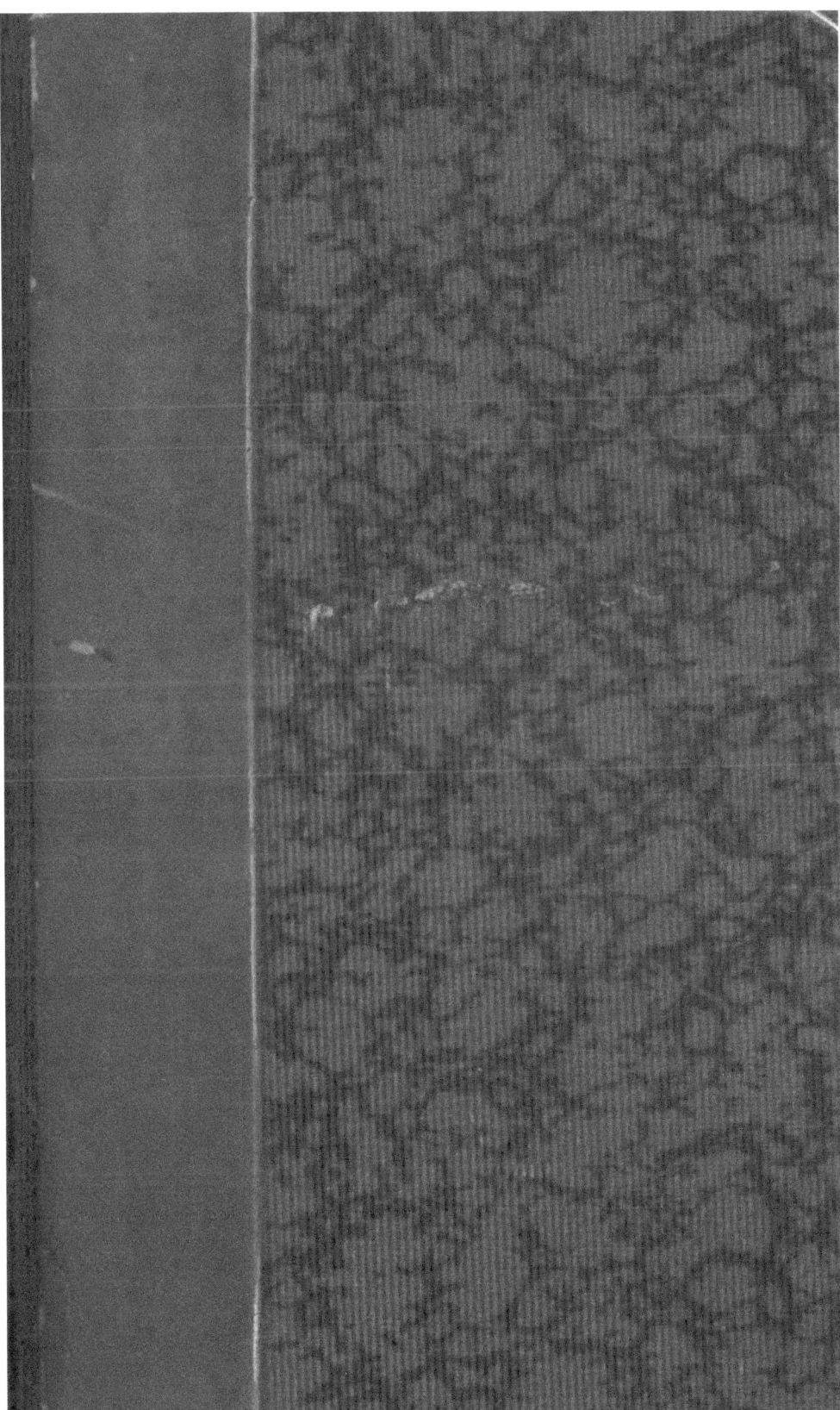

THE STRANGE ADVENTURES

OF

CAPTAIN DANGEROUS:

WHO WAS A SOLDIER, A SAILOR, A MERCHANT, A SPY, A SLAVE
AMONG THE MOORS, A BASHAW IN THE SERVICE
OF THE GRAND TURK,

AND

Died at last in his own House in Hanover Square.

A NARRATIVE IN OLD-FASHIONED ENGLISH.

ATTEMPTED BY

GEORGE AUGUSTUS SALA.

IN THREE VOLUMES.

VOL. III.

LONDON:
TINSLEY BROTHERS, 18, CATHERINE STREET, STRAND.
1863.

LONDON:
SAVILL AND EDWARDS, PRINTERS, CHANDOS STREET,
COVENT GARDEN.

CONTENTS OF VOL. III.

CHAPTER THE SEVENTH.

CHAPTER THE EIGHTH.

CHAPTER THE NINTH AND LAST.

THE STRANGE ADVENTURES

OF

CAPTAIN DANGEROUS.

A Narrative in Old Fashioned English.

———

CHAPTER THE FIRST.

I SEE MUCH OF THE INSIDE OF THE WORLD, AND THEN GO RIGHT ROUND IT.

1748. I was not yet Forty years of age, Hale and Stout, Comely enough,—so said Mistress Prue and many other damsels,—with a Military Education, an approved reputation for Valour, and very little else besides. A gentleman at large, with a purse well-nigh as slender as an ell-wand, and as wobegone as a dried eel-skin. But I was never one that wanted many Superfluities; and having no Friends in the world, was of a most Contented Disposition.

Some trouble, indeed, must I have with that luckless Mistress Prue, the Waiting-Maid—sure, I did the girl no Harm, beyond whispering a little soft nonsense in her ear now and then. But she must needs have a succession of Hysterical Fits after my departure from the Tower, and write me many scores of Letters couched in the most Lamentable Rigmarole, threatening to throw herself into Rosamond's Pond in St. James's Park (then a favourite Drowning-Place for Disconsolate Lovers), with many other non-sensical Menaces. But I was firm to my Determination to do her no harm, and therefore carefully abstained from answering any of her letters. She did not break her heart; but (being resolved to wed one that wore the King's cloth) she married Miles Bandolier about three months after my Departure, and broke his head, ere the Honeymoon was over, with a Bed-staff. A most frivolous Quean this, and I well rid of her.

Coming out of the Tower, I took lodgings for a season in Great Ryder Street, St.

James's, and set up for a Person of Pleasure. There were many Military Officers of my Acquaintance who honoured me with their company over a Bottle, for even as a Tower Warder I had been a kind of a Gentleman, and there was no treating me as one of base Degree. They laughed somewhat at my Brevet rank of Captain, and sometimes twitted me as to what Regiment I was in; but I let them laugh, so long as they did not go too far, when I would most assuredly have shown them, by the length of my Blade, not only what Regiment I belonged to, but what Mettle I was of. By favour of some of my Martial Friends, I was introduced to a favourite Coffee-House, the "Ramilies," in Jermyn Street ('tis Slaughter's, in St. Martin's Lane, now, that the Soldier-Officers do most use); and there we had many a pleasant Carouse, and, moreover, many a good game at cards; at the which, thanks to the tuition of Mr. Hodge, when I was in Mr. Pinchin's service, I was a passable adept, being able to hold my own and More, in almost every Game that is to be found in Hoyle. And so our card-playing did result, not only to mutual pleasure, but to my especial Profit; for I was very lucky. But I declare that I always played fair; and if any man doubted the strict probity of my proceeding, there was then, as there is now, my Sword to vindicate my Honour.

'Tis ill-living, however, on Gambling. Somehow or another the Money you win at Cards——I would never touch Dice, which are too chancy, liable to be Sophisticated, and, besides, sure to lead to Brawling, Stabbing, and cracking of Crowns——this Money, gotten over Old Nick's back, I say, never seems to do a Man any Good. 'Tis light come, and light go; and the Store of Gold Pieces that glitter so bravely when you sweep them off the green cloth seems, in a couple of days afterwards, to have turned to dry leaves, like the Magician's in the Fairy Tale. Excepting Major Panton, who built the Street and the Square which bear his name out of One Night's Profit at the Pharoah table, can you tell me of one habitual Gambler who has been able to realise anything substantial out of his Winnings? No, no; a Hand at Cards is all very well, and 'tis pleasant to win enough to pay one's Reckoning, give a Supper to the Loser, and have a Frisk upon Town afterwards; but I do abhor your steady, systematic Gamblers, with their restless eyes, quivering lips, hair bristling under their wigs, and twitching fingers, as they watch the Game. Of course, when Cards are played, you must play for Money. As to playing for Love, I would as soon play for nutshells or cheese-parings. But the whole business is too feverish and exciting for a Man of warm temperament. 'Tis killing work when your Bed and Raiment, your Dinner and your Flask, depend on the turn up of a card. And so I very speedily abandoned this line of life.

'Twas necessary, nevertheless, for something to be done to bring Grist to the Mill. About this time it was a very common practice for Great Noblemen—notably those who were in any way addicted to pleasure,

and ours was a mighty Gay Nobility thirty
or forty years since—to entertain Men of
Honour, Daring, and Ability, cunning in the
use of their Swords, and exceedingly discreet
in their conversations, to attend them upon
their private affairs, and render to them
Services of a kind that required Secrecy as
well as Courage.   One or two Duels in
Hyde Park and behind Montagu House,
in which I had the honour to be concerned
as Second,—and in one of which I engaged
the Second of my Patron's Adversary, and
succeeded, by two dexterous side slices, in
Quincing his face as neatly as a housewife
would slice Fruit for a Devonshire Squab
Pie,—gained me the notice of some of the
Highest Nobility, to whom I was otherwise recommended by the easiness of my
Manners, and the amenity of my Language.
The young Earl of Modesley did in particular affect me, and I was of Service to
his Lordship on many most momentous and
delicate Occasions.   For upwards of Six
Months I was sumptuously entertained in
his Lordship's Mansion in Red Lion Square;

—a Kind of Hospitality, indeed, which he was most profuse in the dispensation of:— there being at the same time in the House a French Dancing-Master, an Italian Singer, a Newmarket Horse-Jockey, and a Domestic Chaplain, that had been unfrocked for too much fighting of Cocks and drinking of Cider with clowns at his Vicarage; but to whom the Earl of Modesley was always a fast friend. Unfortunate Young Nobleman! He died of a malignant Fever at Avignon, just before attâining his Thirtieth Year! His intentions towards me were of the most Bounteous Description; and he even, being pleased to say that I was a good-looking Fellow enough, and come to an Age when it behoved me to be settled in Life, proposed that I should enter in the bonds of Wedlock with one Miss Jenny Lightfoot, that had formerly been a Milliner in Liquorpond Street, but who, when his Lordship introduced me to her, lived in most splendid Lodgings under the Piazza, Covent Garden, and gave the handsomest Chocolate Parties to the Young Nobility that ever were seen. So Boundless was his Lordship's generosity that he offered to bestow a portion of Five Hundred Pounds on Miss Lightfoot if she would become Madame Dangerous—said portion to be at my absolute disposal—and to give me besides a long Lease at a Peppercorn Rent of a Farm of his in Wiltshire. The Match, however, came to nothing. I was not yet disposed to surrender my Liberty; and, indeed, the Behaviour of Miss Lightfoot, while the Treaty of Alliance between us was being discussed, did not augur very favourably for our felicity in the Matrimonial State. Indeed, she was pleased to call me Rogue, Gambler, Bully, Led Captain, and many other uncivil names. She snapped off the silver hilt of my dresssword (presented to me after I had fought the Second in Hyde Park), and obstinately refused to restore that gewgaw to me, telling me that she had given it to her Landlady (one Mother Bishopsbib, a monstrous Fat Woman, that was afterwards Carted, and stood in the Pillory in Spring

Gardens, for evil practices) in part payment for rent-owing. Moreover, she wilfully spoilt my best periwig by overturning a Chocolate Mill thereupon; and otherwise so misconducted herself that I bade her a respectful Farewell,—she leaving the marks of her Nails on my face as a parting Gift,— and told my Lord Modesley that I would as lief wed a Roaring Dragon as this Termagant of the Piazza. This Refusal brought about a Rupture between myself and my Lord. He was imprudent enough to talk about my Ingratitude, to tell me that the very coat on my back was bought and paid for with his Money, and to threaten to have me kicked out of doors by two of his Tall Lacqueys. But I speedily let him have a piece of my Mind. "My Lord," says I, going up to him, and thrusting my face full in his, "you will be pleased to know that I am a Gentleman, whose ancestors were ennobled centuries before your rascally grandfather got his peerage for turning against the true King."

He began to murmur something (as many

have done before when my blood was up, and I have mentioned Royalty) about my being " a Jacobite."

" I'll Jacobite your jacket for you, you Jackadandy!" I retorted.   " You have most foully insulted me.   I know your Lordship's ways well.   If I sent you a cartel, you and your whippersnapper Friends would sneer at it, because I am poor, and fling Led Captain in my teeth.   You won't fight with a poor Gentleman of the Sword.   I am too much of a Man of Honour to waylay you at night, and give you the private Stab, as you deserve; but so sure as you are your father's son, if you don't make me this instant a Handsome Apology, I will cudgel you till there is not a whole bone in your body."

The young Ruffian—he was not such a coward as Squire Pinchin, but rather murderous—makes no more do, but draws upon me.   I caught up a quarter-staff that lay handy (for we were always exercising ourselves at athletic amusements), struck the weapon from his grasp, and hit him a sounding thwack across the shins that brought him down upon his marrow-bones.

"Below the Belt!" he cries out, holding up his hands. "Foul! foul!"

"Foul be hanged!" I answered. "I'm not going to fight, but to Beat You;" and I rushed upon him, shortening the Staff, and would have belaboured him Soundly, but that he saw it was no use contending against John Dangerous, and very humbly craved a parley. He Apologised as I had Demanded, and lent me Twenty Guineas, and we parted on the most friendly terms.

This Lord essayed, notwithstanding, to do me much harm in Town, saying that I had used him with black Cruelty, had re-requited his many favours with gross Treachery, and the like Falsehoods, until I was obliged to send him a Message to this purport: that unless he desisted, I should be obliged to keep my promise as to the Cudgel. Upon which he presently surceased. So much meanness had he, even, as to fudge up a pretended debt of nineteen guineas against me as for money lent, for the which I was arrested by bailiffs and conveyed——being taken at Jonathan's——to a vile spunging-house in Little Bell Alley, Moorfields; but the keeper of the House stood my friend, and procured a Bail for me in the shape of an Honest Gentleman, who was to be seen every day about Westminster Hall with a straw in his shoe, and for a crown and a dinner at the eating-house would suddenly become worth five hundred a year, or at least swear himself black in the face that such was his estate:——which was all that was required. And when it came to justifying of Bail before the Judges, what so easy as to hire a suit of clothes in Monmouth Street, and send him into court fully equipped as a reputable gentleman ? However, there was no occasion for this, for on the very night of my enlargement I won fifty guineas at the tables; and walking very Bold to my Lord's House, sends up the nineteen guineas to my Lord with a note, asking to what lawyer I should pay the cost of suit, and whether I should wait upon him at his Levee for a receipt. On the which he, still with the fear of a cudgelling before his eyes, sends me down a Receipt in Full, *and the Money back to boot,* begging me to trouble myself in no way about the lawyer; which, I promise you, I did not. And so an end of this troublesome acquaintance,—a profitable one enough to me while it lasted. As for Miss Jenny, her Behaviour soon became as light as her name. I have heard that she got into trouble about a Spanish Merchant that was flung down stairs and nigh killed, and that but for the Favour of Justice Cogwell, who had a hankering for her, 'twould have been a Court-Job. Afterwards I learnt that she had been seen beating Hemp in Bridewell in a satin sack laced with silver; and I warrant that she was fain to cry, "Knock! oh, good Sir Robert, knock!" many a time before the Blue-coated Beadles on court day had done swingeing of her.

There are certain periods in the life even of the most fortunate man when his Luck is at a desperately low ebb,—when everything seems to go amiss with him,—when nothing that he can turn his hand to prospers,— when friends desert him, and the companions of his sunshiny days chide him for not having made better use of his opportunities, —when, Do what he will, he cannot avert the Black Storm,—when Ruin seems impending, and Catastrophe is on the cards,— when he is Down, in a word, and the despiteful are getting ready to gibe at him in his Misfortune, and to administer unto him the last Kick. These times of Trial and Bitter Travail ofttimes strike one who has just attained Middle age,—the Halfway-House of Life; and then, 'tis the merest chance in the world whether he will be enabled to pick himself up again, or be condemned for evermore to poverty and contumely,—to the portion of weeds and outworn faces. I do confess that about this period of my career things went very badly with me, and that I was grievously hard-driven, not alone to make both ends meet, but to discover anything that could have its ending in a Meal of Victuals. I have heard

that some of the greatest Prelates, States-
men, Painters, Captains, and Merchants—I
speak not of Poets, for it is their eternal
portion, seemingly, to be born, to live, and
to Die Poor—have suffered the like straits
at some time or another of their lives.
Many times, however, have I put it on
record in these pages, that Despair and I
were never Bedfellows. As for Suicide, I
do condemn it, and abhor it utterly, as the
most cowardly, Dishonest, and unworthy
Method to which a Man can resort that he
may rid himself of his Difficulties. To
make a loathsome unhandsome corpse of
yourself, and deny yourself Christian Burial,
nay, run the risk of crowner's quest, and
interment at the meeting of four cross-roads
with a Stake driven through your Heart.
Oh, 'tis shameful! Hang yourself, forsooth!
why should you spend money in threepenny
cord, when Jack Ketch, if you deserve it,
will hang you for nothing, and the County
find the rope? Take poison! why, you are
squeamish at accepting physic from the
doctor, which may possibly do you good.

Why, then, should you swallow a vile mess which you are *certain* must do you harm? Fall upon your sword, as Tully—I mean Brutus—or some of those old Romans, were wont to do when the Game was up! In the first place, I should like to see the man, howsoever expert a fencer, who could so tumble on his own blade and kill himself. 'Tis easier to swallow a sword than to fall upon one, and the first is quite as much a Mountebank's Trick as t'other. Blow your brains out! A mighty fine climax truly, to make a Horrible Mess all over the floor, and frighten the neighbours out of their wits, besides, as a waggish friend of mine has it, rendering yourself stone-deaf for life. If it comes to powder and ball, why, a Man of courage would much sooner blow out somebody else's Brains instead of his own.

I did not, I am thankful to say, want Bread during this my time of ill luck; and I never parted with my sword; but sure it is that Jack Dangerous was woundily pushed, and had to adopt many extraordinary shifts for a livelihood. Item: I engaged myself to one Mr. O'Teague, an Irishman, that had been a pupil of the famous Mr. Figg, Master of the Noble Art of Self-Defence, at his Theatre of Arms, on the right hand side of the Oxford Road, near Adam and Eve Court. Mr. Figg was, as is well known, the very Atlas of the Sword; and Mr. O'Teague's body was a very Mass of Scars and Cicatrices gotten in hand-to-hand conflicts with the broadsword on the public stage. He had once presumed to rival Mr. Figg, whence arose a cant saying of the time, " A fig for the Irish;" but having been honourably vanquished by him, even to the slicing of his nose in two pieces, the cracking of his crown in sundry places, and the scoring of his body as though it had been a Loin of Pork for the Bakehouse, he was taken into his service, and became a principal figure in all the grand gladiatorial encounters, at wages of forty shillings a week and his meat. As for Mr. Figg himself, who was as good at backsword as at broadsword, at quarter-staff as at foil, and at fisticuffs as any one of them,—to say nothing of his Cornish wrestling,—I saw him once, and shall never forget him. There was a Majesty blazed in his countenance and shone in all his actions beyond all I ever beheld. His right leg bold and firm; and his Left, which could hardly ever be disturbed, gave him the surprising advantages he so often proved, and struck his Adversary with Despair and Panic. He had that peculiar way of stepping in, in a Parry, which belongs to the Grand School alone; he knew his arm, and its just time of moving; put a firm faith in that, and never let his foe escape a parry. He was just as much as great a master as any I ever saw, as he was a greater judge of time and Measure. It was his method, when he fought in his Amphitheatre, to send round to a select number of his scholars to borrow a shirt for the ensuing combat, and seldom failed of half-a-dozen of superfine Holland from his prime Pupils. Most of the young Nobility and Gentry made it a part of their education to march under his warlike banner. Most of his Scholars were at every battle, and were sure to exult at their great master's victories; every person supposing he saw the wounds his shirt received. Then Mr. Figg would take an opportunity to inform his Lenders of the charm their Linen had received, with an offer to send the garments home; but he seldom received any other answer than " Hang you, keep it." A most ingenious and courageous person, and immeasurably beyond all his competitors, such as O'Teague, Will Holmes, Felix Maguire, Broughton, Sutton, and the like.

Many good bouts with all kinds of weapons did we have at Mr. O'Teague's theatre, which was down a Stable-yard behind Newport Market, not far from Orator Henley's chapel. The shirt manoeuvre we tried over and over again with varying success; but we found it in the end impossible to preserve order among our Patrons, the greater part of whom were Butchers; and I am fain to admit that many of these unctuous sky-blue jerkins could fight as well as we. Then Mr. O'Teague was much given to drinking, and in his potations quarrelsome. 'Twas all very well fighting on a stage for profit, and with the chance of applause, a clean shirt, and perchance a Right Good Supper given to us by our admirers afterwards at some neighbouring Tavern; but I never could see the humour of Swashbuckling for nothing, and without occasion; and as my Employer was somewhat too prompt to call in cold iron when his Head was so Hot, I shook hands with him, and bade him find another assistant. This was the Mr. O'Teague that was afterwards so unfortunate as to be hanged at Tyburn for devalising a gentleman at Roehampton. Great interest was made to save him, his very prosecutor (who knew not at the first his assailant, or that he had been driven to the road by hard times) heading the signatures to a petition for him. But 'twas all in vain. He made a beautiful end of it in a fine white nightcap fringed; and his funeral was attended by some of the most eminent swordsmen in town, who had a gallant set-to afterwards for the benefit of his widow. 'Tis sad to think of the numbers of brave men that I have known, and how many of them are Hanged.

About this time I was much with the Players, but misliked them exceedingly; and although numbers of brilliant offers were made to me, I could not be persuaded to try the sock and buskin. Hard as were the names by which my enemies would sometimes call me, I could never abide that of Rogue and Vagabond, and such, by Act of Parliament, was the player at that time. No, I said, whatever straits I am driven to, I will be a Soldier of Fortune, and Captain Dangerous to the last.

Of my Adventure with Madam Taffetas the Widow, I am not disposed to say much. Indeed, until my being finally settled, and made the Happiest Man upon earth by my union with the departed Saint who was the mother of my Lilias, it must be admitted that my commerce with the Sex was mostly of the unluckiest description. I have been used most shamefully by women; but it behoves me not to complain, seeing how much felicity I was permitted to enjoy in my latter days. This much, however, I will discreetly set down. That meeting Madam Taffetas in a side box at Drury Lane playhouse, She was pleased to accept my Addresses, and to inform me that my conversation was in the highest degree tasteful to her. I entertained her very handsomely —indeed much beyond my means, for I was very heavily in debt for necessaries, and I could scarcely walk the streets without apprehensions of the grim Sergeant with his capias. Madam Taffetas was an exceedingly comely person, amazingly well dressed, and, as I was given to understand, in very prosperous circumstances. She kept an Italian Warehouse by the Sign of The two Olive Posts, in the broad part of the Strand, almost opposite to Exeter Change, and sold all sorts of Italian Silks, Lustrings, Satins, Paduasoys, Velvets, Damasks, Fans, Leghorn Hats, Flowers, Violin Strings, Books of Essences, Venice Treacle, Balsams, Florence Cordials, Oil, Olives, Anchovies, Capers, Vermicelli, Bologna Sausages, Parmesan Cheese, Naples

Soap, and similar delicate cates from foreign parts. All her friends put her down as a forty-thousand-pounder. In Brief, she professed to be satisfied with my gentility and Ancient Lineage, though worldly goods I had none to offer her. All congratulated me on my Good Fortune; and not wanting to make any unnecessary bustle about the affair, we took coach one fine Monday morning down to Fleet Market, and were married by a Fleet parson—none other, indeed, than my old friend Chaplain Hodge, who had taken to this way of life and found it very profitable, marrying his twenty or thirty couple a week, when Business was brisk, at fees varying from five guineas to seven-and-sixpence, and from a dozen of Burgundy to half a pint of Geneva. But 'twas a rascally business, the venerable man said, and he sorely longed for the good old days when he, and I, and Squire Pinchin, made the Grand Tour together. Alas, for that poor little man! His Reverence told me that he had gone from bad to worse; that his Mamma had married a knavish lawyer, who so be-

wildered Mr. Pinchin with Mortgages, and
Deeds of Gift, and Loans at usurious interest, that he got at last the whole of his property from him, brought him in many thousands in debt besides, and, after keeping him
for three years locked up and half-starved
in the Compter, was only forced to consent
to his enlargement when the unhappy little
man—whose head was never of the strong-
est, and his wits always going a wool-gather-
ing—went stark-staring mad, and was, by
the City charity, removed to Bedlam Hospital in Moorfields.   There he raved for a
time, imagining himself to be the Pope of
Rome, with a paper-cap for a tiara, an ell-
wand for a crosier, a blanket for a rochet,
and bestowing his blessings on the other
Maniacs with much force and vehemence;
and there, poor demented creature, he died
in the year 1740.

Much better would it have been for me,
had I gone straight off my Head and had
been sent to howl in Bedlam, than that I
should have married that same thievish cata-
maran, Madam Taffetas.   Surely never

Madman deserved a Dark House and a Whip more than I did for that most foolishly contracted union. I defy Calumny to prove that I ever used anything approaching false Representations in this matter. I told her plainly that my Hand, Sword, and Deep Devotion were all I had to offer, and that for mere vile pounds, shillings, and pence, and other Mercantile Arrangements, I must look to her. Absolutely I borrowed ten pieces, although I was then at a very Low Ebb, to defray the expenses of the wedding Treat, which was done most handsomely at the Bible and Crown, in Pope's Head Alley, Cornhill. "Now then," I said to myself, as we came home towards the Strand (for we were resolved to have no foolish honeymooning in the Country, but to remain in town and keep an eye to Business)—"now then, Jack Dangerous, thou art at last Married and Settled, and need trouble thyself no more about the cares and anxieties of money-grubbing and bread-getting. Thou art tiled-in handsomely, Jack; thatched and fenced, and girt about with Comfort and Respectability.   Thy hat is on, and thy house is covered." Alas, poor fool! alas, triply distilled zany and egregiously doting idiot! No sooner did a Hackney coach set us down at the Leghorn Warehouse in the broad part of the Strand, than we found Margery the maid and Tom the shopboy in a great confusion of tears on the threshold; and immediately afterwards we heard that during our absence to get married, Bailiffs had made their entrance, and seized all the Merchandise for a bill owing by Madam Taffetas to her Factor of Seven Hundred Pounds. The false Quean that I was wedded to was hopelessly bankrupt, and with the greatest impudence in the world she calls upon me to pay the Money; the Bailiffs adding, with a grin, that to their knowledge she owed much more than their Execution stood for, and that no doubt, so soon as it was bruited abroad that I was her Husband, the Sheriff of Middlesex would have something to say to me in the way of a capias against my person.   In vain did I Rave and Swear, and endeavour to show that I could in no way be held liable for Debts which I had never contracted. Such, I was told, was the Law; and such it remains to this day, to the Great Scandal' of justice, and the detriment of Gentlemen cavalieros who may be entrapped into marrying vulgar Adventuresses whom they deem Gentlewomen of Property, and who turn out instead to be not worth two-pence-halfpenny in the world. Nor were words wanting to add dire Insult to this astounding Injury; for Madam Taffetas, now Dangerous, as I groaningly remembered, must needs call me Mercenary Rascal, Shuffling Pickthank, Low-minded Fortune-hunter, and the like unkind names.

Madam Dangerous indeed! But I am thankful to Providence that the title she assumed very soon fell away from her, and that I was once more left free and Independent. For whilst we were in the very midst of Hot Dispute and violent Recrimination comes a great noise at the door as though some one were striving to Batter it down. And then Margery the maid and Tom the shop-lad began to howl and yelp again, crying out Murder and thieves, and that they were undone, the Bailiffs smoking their Pipes and drinking their Beer meanwhile, as though they enjoyed the Humours of the Scene hugely, and my wicked wife now pretending to faint, and now making at me with the avowed Design of tearing my eyes out.   Presently comes lurching and staggering into the room a Great Hulking Brute of a Man that was attired like a Sea Captain; and this Roystering Tarpaulin makes up without more ado to my Precious Partner, gives her two sounding Busses on either side of her cheeks, and salutes her as his wife.

" Your wife!" I cried, starting up; "why, she's my wife!   I married her this very morning, and to my sorrow, before Parson Hodge, the Couple-Beggar, at the Fleet."

" That may be, Brother," answers the Sea Captain, with drunken gravity; "but she's my wife, for all that.   You married her this morning, you say.   I married her five years ago, at Horsleydown, and in the Parish church.   I've got the 'Stifficate to prove it; and though I say it that shouldn't, there's not a Finer woman, with a neater ankle and such a Devil of a temper, to be found 'twixt Beachy Head and Cape Horn."

" A fig for both of you," bellows Madam Taffetas, who had gone into one of her Sham Faints in the arm-chair, but was now conveniently recovered again. "If I'm married to both of you—to you, you pitiless Grampus" (this was to the Sea Captain), "and to you, Ruffian, Bully, and Stabster" (this was to me), "I'm married to somebody else, and my real Husband is a Gentleman, who, if he were here, would quoit the pair of you into the street from Exeter Change to the Fox under the Hill."

She said this in one Scream, and then Fainted, or pretended to Faint again.

" Brother," said the Sea Captain to me, staggering a little (for he confessed to having much mixed punch under hatches), but still very grave,—" brother, I think as how it's clear that we're both of us d——d fools, and d——d lucky fellows at the same time."

"Amen!" cries one of the Bailiffs, with a guffaw.

"*You* belay," remarked the Captain, turning towards the vermin of Law with profound disdain. "Brother" (turning to me), "is the Press out?"

"What do you mean?" I inquired. "You know that there's no warrant for press-gangs in this part of the Liberties of Westminster."

"Liberty be Hanged!" quoth the Sea Captain. "If there was any liberty, there couldn't be a press, for which I don't care a groat, for I'm a master mariner. This is what I mean. Is them landlubbers there part of a press-gang? Are you trápped, brother? Are you in the bilboes? Are you in any danger of being put under hatches?"

"Why," upspoke one of the Bailiffs, answering for me, "the truth is that we are Sheriff's Sergeants, and have made seizure, according to due writ of *fi. fa.* of this worthy lady's goods. We've nothing at all against the gentleman who says that he married her this morning; but as you said that you married her five years ago, it's very likely that we, or some of our mates, shall have something to say to you, in the form of parchment, between this and noon to-morrow."

" Very well," answers the Strange Seaman. " You speak like a Man o' War's chaplain, some Lies and some Lingo, but all of it d——d Larned. Have you got ere a drop of rum, brother?"

" There's nothing here but some Three-Thread Swipes," responds Mr. Bailiff; " and, indeed, we were waiting until the gentleman treated us to something better."

" Then," continues the Captain, " you shall have some rum. Younker, go and fetch these gentlemen some liquor;" and he flings a crown to the shop-lad. " You may drink your grog and blow your baccy," he went on, " as long as ever you like, and much good may it do you. And as for you, Pig-faced Nan,"——in this uncivil manner did he address the false Madam Taffetas,—— " you may go to bed, or to the Devil, 'zactly

as you choose, and settle your Business with
the Bailiffs in the morning 'zactly as you
like. And you and I, brother," he wound
up, taking me by the arm in quite a friendly
manner, " will just go and take our grog
and blow our baccy in peace and quietness,
and thank the Lord for it."

All this he said with great thickness and
indistinctness of utterance, but with an im-
movable gravity of countenance. I never
saw a Man who was manifestly so Drunk
speak so sensibly, and behave himself in
such a proper manner in my life.

As he turned on his heel to leave the
parlour where all this took place, I saw one
of the Bailiffs rise stealthily as if to follow
us.

" Belay there!" the Captain cried, ad-
vancing his mahogany paw in a warning
manner. " Hold hard, shipmates. I'm a
peaceable man, and aboard they call me
Billy the Lamb; but, by the Lord Harry,
if I catch you sneaking about, or trying to
find out where I and this noble gentleman
be agoing, I'm blest if I don't split your skull

in two with this here speaking-trumpet." And so saying the Captain produced a very long tin tube, such as Mariners carry to make their voices heard at a distance at sea, but which they generally have aboard, and do not carry with them in their walks.

The Bailiffs were sensible men, and forbore to intermeddle with us any more. So we marched out of the House, it being now about nine o'clock at night; and, upon my word, from that moment to this, I never set eyes upon Madam Taffetas, or Dangerous, or Blokes,—for the Sea Captain's name, he afterwards told me, was Blokes,— or whatever her real name was. It is very certain that she used me most scandalously, and cruelly betrayed the trusting confidence of one that was not only a Bachelor, but an Orphan.

Captain Blokes was a strange character. We had a grand Carouse that night, he paying the Shot like a gentleman; and over our flowing Bowls, he told me that he had long had suspicions of his wife's real character; and was, indeed, in possession of evidence (though he had kept it secret) to prove that she had given herself in marriage to another man before she had wedded him. And then, through the serving-lad, he had heard that very morning, on his coming into the Pool from Gravesend and Foreign Parts, that Madam, who thought him in China at least, and hoped him Dead, was about to enter into Wedlock once again; so that, determined to have Sport, he had well Primed himself with Punch, and lurked about the neighbourhood until Monsieur Tomfool and his Spouse (by which I mean myself, although no other man should call me so) had come home from the Fleet. And so all the Crying, and Lord ha' Mercies, of the Wench and the Boy, were all subterfuges; and they knew very well, the sly rogues, that the Sea Captain would soon be to the Fore.

Nothing would suit him after this but that we should have Supper at the King of Prussia's Head, in the Savoy, and, as I had given up my Lodgings as not Grand enough for me on the eve of my wedding, and the Vessel of which he was Commander was lying in the Pool, that we should have Beds —at his charges—at the same Tavern; and, indeed, your Seafaring Men, although rough enough, and smelling woundily of tar and bilge-water, are the most Hospitable Creatures breathing; and that makes Me so free with my Money when there is a treat afoot; albeit I can, without Vanity, declare myself Amphibious, for I have seen as much service by Sea as by Land, and have always approved myself a Gentleman of Courage, Honour, and Discretion, on both Elements.

The next morning, after a Nip of Aquavitæ, to clear the Cobwebs out of our throats, we went down to Billingsgate, where we saw my old humorous acquaintances, Brandy Sall, the fishwife, and the humorous porter, the Duke of Puddledock; likewise a merry Wag that did porterage work for the Fish Factors in the Market, and thereby seemed to have caught somewhat of the form of the fish beneath which his shoulders were continually groaning, so that all who could take that liberty with him called him Cod's Head and Shoulders. Here we breakfasted on new Oysters and Fried Flounders, with a lappet of Kippered Salmon, for Goodman Thirst's sake, and a rare bowl of hot Coffee, which made us relish a Jug of Punch afterwards in a highly jocund manner. And then we fell to conversation; and I, who had nothing to Conceal, and nothing to be Ashamed of, did recount those of my Adventures which I deemed would be most diverting (for I forbore to tell him those which were tedious and uneventful) to Captain Blokes. And he, not to be behind-hand in frank confidence, told me how many years he had been at sea; how many merchant vessels he had commanded; and what Luck he had had in his divers Trading Adventures. Likewise, that he was now under engagement with some very worthy Merchants of Bristol, to man, equip, and command a vessel called the *Marquis*, which, in company with two others, the *Hope* and the *Delight*, were about to undertake a Cruising Voyage round the World. Finding from my speech that I was not wholly unaccustomed to the Sea, and being made acquainted with what I had done in the West Indies and elsewhere, Captain Blokes was pleased to say that I was the very man for him, if I would join him. And at this time, in verity, it seemed as though nothing could suit me better; for my Resources were quite exhausted, and I was brought very Low. So, after some further parley, and a good Beefsteak and Onions, and a bottle of Portugee Wine for dinner, we went to the Scrivener's in Thames Street, by the name of Pritchett, that was Agent for the Company of Merchant Adventurers at Bristol; and an Agreement was drawn up, by which, for Fifty Shillings a month pay, all due rations and allowances, and a certain proportion of the profits to be divided among the Ship's Company at the termination of our Adventure, I bound myself to serve Captain Blokes as Secretary and Purser of the ship *Marquis*.

"Which means," says he, when we had taken a Dram and shaken hands on signing

articles, "that you are to Write, Fight,
Drink, and keep Accompts, play put with
me in the Cabin, assist me in preserving the
Discipline of the Ship, sing a good song
when you are called upon, help the Doctor
to take care of the sick, and see that the
Steward don't steal the Grog and Tobacco;
and if you'll stick to me, by the Lord Harry,
Billy Blokes will stick to you.   I like you
because you were such a d——d fool as to go
and marry that old woman."

The next day we took Coach at the Swan,
by Paddington Church, for Bristol, and two
days afterwards arrived at that great and
flourishing Mercantile city. Nothing worthy
of note on the road; the Highwaymen, that
were wont to be so troublesome, being mostly
put down, owing to Justice Fielding and De
Vit's stringent measures.   We were much
beset with gangs of wild Irish coming over
from their own country a-harvesting in our
fertile fields; and those gentry were like to
have bred a riot, quarrelling with the English
husbandmen at Stow.   Being at Bristol,
comfortably housed at the Bible and Crown

in Wine Street,——the landlord much given
to swearing, but one of the best hands at
making of Mum that ever I knew,——Captain
Blokes had great work in settling business
with the Company of Merchant Adventurers
and Alderman Quarterbutt, their President.
As it seems we were at war with the French
and Spaniards, the *Marquis* (burden about
320 tons) was to carry twenty-six guns and
a complement of 108 men, letters of marque
being granted to us by private Commission,
with secret instruction as to Prizes and
Plunder, so that the disposal of both should
redound to the advantage of the Mariners,
the Profit of our Employers, and the honour
of His Majesty's arms. We had nigh double
the usual complement of officers usual in
private ships, to prevent Mutinies, which
ofttimes happen in long voyages, and that
we might have a large provision for a succession of officers in case of Mortality. In
the *Marquis* we had Captain Blokes, com-
mander-in-chief of the whole Armament, a
Mariner; a Second Captain, who was a Dr.
of Physick, and also acted as President of

our Committee (having much book-learning), and Commander of the Marines; two Leftenants; a Sailing Master; a Pilot that was well acquainted with the South Seas, having been in those latitudes twice before; a Surgeon and his Mate, or Loblolly Boy; Self as Secretary and Purser; two young lawyers, designed to act as Midshipmen; Giles Cash, as Reformado,—that was the title of courtesy given to those who were sent to sea in lieu of being hanged; a Gunner and his crew; a Boatswain, cooper, carpenter, sailmaker, smith, and armourer, ship's corporal, Sergeant of Marines, cook; a Negro that could shave and play the fiddle; and the Ship's company as aforesaid, one-third of whom were foreigners of every nation under the Sun; and of those that were His Majesty's subjects, many Tinkers, Tailors, Haymakers, Pedlars, &c.—a terribly mixed Gang, requiring much three-strand cord to keep 'em in order.

On the 2nd August, 1748, we weighed from King's Road, by Bristol, and at ten at night, having very little wind, anchored be-

tween the Holms and Minehead. Coming
on a fresh gale at S.E. and E.S.E., we ran
by Minehead at six in the morning. Next
day the wind veered to N.E. and E.N.E.;
on the 4th there was but little wind, and
smooth water; on the 5th we saw Land;
and finding that we had overshot our port,
which was Cork, came to an anchor at noon
off the two rocks near Kinsale. At eight
at night we weighed, having a Kinsale Pilot
on board, who was like to have endangered
our safety, the night being dark and foggy,
and the Pilot not understanding his Business; so that he nearly turned us into the
next Bay to the westward of Cork, which
provoked Captain Blokes to chastise him
publicly on the quarter-deck. Our two
consorts got into Cork before us, and we
did not anchor in the Cove until the 7th
August, at three in the afternoon. We
stayed here until the 28th of the month,
getting in stores and provisions, and re-
placing as many of our tailors and haymakers
as we could with real Sailors that could
work the Ship. Our crew, however, were

continually Marrying while we were at Cork, to the great Merriment of Self and Captain Blokes, who had seen enough and to spare of that Game; but they *would* be Spliced, although they expected to sail immediately; among others, there was a Danish man coupled by a Romish Priest to an Irish woman, without understanding a word of each other's language, so that they were forced to use an Interpreter; yet I perceived this pair seemed more afflicted at separation than any of the rest. The Fellow continued melancholy for many days after we were at Sea. The rest, understanding each other and the world better, drank their cans of Flip till the very last Minute, concluded with a health to our good voyage and their next Happy Meeting, and then Departed, quite unconcerned.

We took sailing orders on the 1st of September; and then Captain Blokes discovered to the crew whither we were bound,—that is to say, on a four years' voyage,—in order that, if any Disorders should arise among us, we might exchange our Malcontents

while in company with one of His Majesty's
ships. But no complaint was found on
board the *Marquis*, except from one fellow
who was expected to have been Tithing man
that year in his Parish, and said his wife
would be obliged to pay Forty shillings in
his absence; but seeing all hands satisfied,
he was easily quieted, and drank with the
rest to a prosperous voyage. On the 2nd
September we, having cleaned and tallowed
our ship's five streaks below the Water-line,
the fiddler struck up " Lumps o' Pudding,"
and to follow that " Cold and Raw," the
Ship's company joining chorus with a will,
and so fell down to the Spit End by the
Culloden Man of War, as our two Consorts
had done the Night before. When we came
to the Spit End, Captain Blokes saluted the
Culloden with seven Guns, to which they
returned Five in courtesy, and then we
again Three for thanks. And so com-
menced my Journey round the World.

CHAPTER THE SECOND.

MERCATOR HIS PROJECTION, AND WHAT CAME OF IT.

MEANING simply this, that I have often and often, as a little Lad, gazed upon the Great Map—very yellow, and shiny, and cracked on its canvas mounting it was — of the World, upon Mercator's Projection, and devoutly longed for the day to arrive when it might be my fortune to make a Voyage of Circumnavigation. Such a Map, I remember, hung in the Schoolroom at Gnawbit's; and I have often been cruelly beaten for gazing at it and pondering over it, instead of endeavouring to commit to memory a quantity of Words, the meaning of which I could not for the life of me understand.

Now, indeed, I had got my Desire, and was going round the World in a Ship well

found with Men and Stores, occupying myself a responsible position, and one giving
me some Authority, and enjoying the full
Confidence of my Commander, who was,
both when sober and inebriated (and he
was mostly the latter), one of the most
sagacious men I ever knew. He spoke seldom, and then generally with a Hiccup;
but what he said was always to the Purpose. I doubt not, if Captain Blokes had
been in the Royal Navy, he would by this
time be flying his pendant as Admiral.

'Twould fill a volume to give you a Narrative, however brief, of our Voyage. One
does not go round the World quite so easily
as a Cit taking a Wherry from Lambeth
Walk to Chelsea Reach. No, no, my Masters; there are Perils to encounter, Ob-
stacles to overcome, Difficulties to surmount;
and I flatter myself that Jack Dangerous
was not found wanting when a Stout Heart,
a Strong Hand, and a Clear Head were
needed. I repeat that 'tis impossible for
me to give you an exact Log of so lengthy
a Cruise; and you must needs be content

if I set down a few bare Items of the most notable Things that befell us.

On 11th September we chased a strange Sail, and after three hours came up with her. She proved to be a Swedishman. After firing a couple of shots at full Random at her, to show that we meant Mischief if provoked, and one of which Shots, I believe, passed over her Taffrail, and killed a Black Servant and the Captain's Monkey, Captain Blokes boarded her in his Yall; examined the Master, and searched the Ship for Contraband of War; but not finding any save a suspicious quantity of salted Reindeer's Tongues, our Committee agreed that she could not be considered a lawful Prize; and not being willing to hinder time by carrying her into any Harbour for further Examination, we let her go without the least Embezzlement. The Master gave us a dozen of his Reindeer Tongues, and a piece of dry Rufft Beef; and we presented him with a dozen bottles of Red-streak Cider. But while Captain Blokes and the Doctor of Physic and Self were aboard the Swede taking a social Glass with him, our rascally crew took it into their heads to Mutiny, their Grievance being that the vessel was a Contraband, and ought to be made a Prize of. The plain truth was, that the Rogues thirsted for Plunder. The Boatswain was one of the Mutineers. Him we caused to receive Four Dozen from the hands of his own Mates, and well laid on; about a dozen of the rest we put in Irons, after having Drubbed 'em soundly, and fed 'em upon Bread-and-Water; but at the end of a few days they begged Pardon, and, on promising Amendment, were allowed to return to their Duty.

18th September we came in sight of Pico Teneriffe, bearing S.W. by W., distant about eight leagues. This day we spied a Sail under our Lee Bow, between the Islands of Grand Canaries and Forteventura. She showed us a clean Pair of Heels ; but we gave Chase, and after seven hours came up with her. She proved a Prize, safe enough : a Spanish Bark, about 25 tons, with some 45 Passengers, who rejoiced much when they found we were English, having fancied that we were Turks or Sallee Rovers. Amongst our Prisoners were four Friars, and with them the Padre Guardian of Forteventura, a good, honest old fellow, fat, and given to jollity. Him we made heartily merry, drinking the Spanish King's Health, for naught else would he Toast. After we had made all Snug, we stood to the Westward with our Prize to Teneriffe, to have her ransomed, that is to say, her Hull; for her Cargo was not worth redeeming, being extremely shabby,—one or two Butts of Wine, a Hogshead of Brandy, and other small matters, which we determined to keep for our own use. The Spanish Dons made a mighty pother about paying, pleading that the Trade of these Islands enjoyed an immunity from Privateering by arrangement between his Catholic Majesty and the King of Great Britain, and were even seconded by some English merchants of Teneriffe that were frightened at the thought of the cruel Reprisals the Dons might exercise after we went away, both on their Persons and Properties; for Jack Spaniard is one that, if he cannot have Meal, will have Malt. But we soon let 'em know that Possession was Nine Points of the Law, and that we were resolved to stick to our Prize unless we got Ransom, which they presently agreed to. At eight o'clock the next morning we stood into the Port, close to the Town, and spied a Boat coming off, which proved to be the Deputy Governor, a Spanish Don with as many names as an English pickpocket has Aliases, and one Mr. Harbottle, that was English Vice-Consul. They brought us Wine, Figs, Grapes, Hogs, and other Necessaries, as Ransom in Kind for the Bark; and accordingly we restored her, as also the Prisoners, with as much as we could find of what belonged to their Persons; although, Truth to tell, some of our wild Reformadoes had used them somewhat unhandsomely. All the Books, Crucifixes, Reliques, and other superstitious things, we carefully gave back to the Friars; to the Padre a large Cheese, at which he was much delighted; and to another Religious, who had been stripped nearly as bare as a Robin, a pair of Breeches and a Red Nightcap. And so stood off, giving Three Cheers for King George, and one, with better luck next time, for the King of Spain; and I doubt not that they cursed us heartily that same night in their Churches, for Heretics. Now we had an indifferent good stock of Liquor, to be the better able to endure the Cold when we got to the length of Cape Horn, which, we were informed, had always very Cold Weather near it.

On the 25th, according to custom, we Ducked those that had never passed the Tropic before. The manner of doing it was to reeve a Rope in the Mainyard, to hoist 'em about half-way up to the Yard, and let 'em fall at once into the Water; they being comfortably Trussed by having a Stick 'cross through their Legs, and well fastened to the Rope, that they might not be surprised and let go their Hold. This proved of great use to our Fresh-water Sailors, to recover the Colour of their Skins, which had grown very Black and Nasty. Those that we Ducked in this manner Three Times were about 60; and others that would not undergo it could redeem themselves by a Fine of Half-a-Crown, to be Levied and Spent at a Public Meeting of all the Ships' Companies when we returned to England. The Dutchmen we had on board, and some few English, desired to be Ducked, some six, others eight and ten times, to have the better title for being Treated when they came home.

On the 1st October we made St. Vincent, where our Water began to smell insufferably; so had some Coopers from the *Hope* and *Delight* to make us Casks, and take in a fresh Stock.

On the 3d we sent a boat to St. Antonio, with one of our Gunners' Crew that was a very fair Linguist, to get Truck for our Prize Goods what we wanted; they having plenty of Cattle, Pigs, Goats, Fowls, Melons, Potatoes, Limes, and ordinary Brandies, Tobacco, Indian Corn, &c. Our people were very meanly stocked with Clothes; yet we were forced to watch our men very narrowly, and Punish some of 'em smartly, to prevent their selling what Garments they had, for mere Trifles, to the Negroes.

We got all we wanted by the 8th; but our Linguist gave us leg-bail; and as he was much given to telling of Lies, we did not go to the pains of sending a party of Marines on shore after him. This is the place whither the Blacks come from St. Nicholas to make Oil of Turtle for the anointing of their Nasty Bodies withal. There was much good Green Turtle at this time of the year, which made me think of my old Jamaica days; but our men, in a body, refused to eat it, much preferring Salt Junk.

Item.—Many Flying Fish about here.

Nothing more worthy of note till the 22d October, when Mr. Page, Second Mate, made an attack on his superior officer, the Doctor of Physic, with a Marline-spike; and, but for a very large Periwig he wore, which was accounted odd in one having a Maritime Command, would have finished him. Mr. Page was had to the Forecastle and clapped in the Bilboes, and Captain Blokes was for

Hanging him off-hand as an Example to the rest; but I, as Secretary, pointed out to him that there was no Power of Life and Death in our Instructions, and that it would be folly to run the risk of a Præmunire when we made Home again. With much trouble I succeeded in dissuading him from his Design: so that the Mate was only lashed to the Main-gears and soundly Drubbed. Fair, pleasant Weather, and a fresh Gale. One that had secreted a Peruke, and a pair of scarlet Stockings with silver Clocks, out of the plunder of the Spanish Bark, did also receive Rib-roasting enough (this was on a Sunday, after Prayers) to last him for a fortnight.

On the 10th of November, after a terrific Tornado and Thunder and Lightning, that frightened some of our Tailors and Hay-makers half into Fits, we came to an Anchor in 22-fathom water, in a sandy bay off the land of Brazil. Caught some Tortoises for their Shells, for they have too strong a taste to be Eatable. A Portugee boat came from a Cove in the Island of Grande, on our

Starboard side, and said they had been robbed by the French not long since. Captain Blokes, the Doctor, and Self went ashore to Angre de Keys, as it is called in Sea-Draughts; but, as the Portugee call it, Nostra Senora de la Concepcion, a small village about three leagues distant, to wait on the Governor, and make him a present of Butter and Cheese. As we neared the shore, the People, taking us for Mounseers, fired a few Musquetoons at us, which did us no Hurt; and when they found out who we were, they very Humbly Begged our Pardon. The Friars invited us to their Convent, and told us they had been so often stripped and abused by King Lewis's frog-eating Subjects, that they were obliged to take measures to Defend themselves; and, indeed, 'twas these said Padres who had fired at us. The Governor was gone to Rio Janeiro, a city about twelve leagues distant, but was expected back next day. We got our empty Casks ashore, and sent our Carpenter, with a friendly Portugee, to look out Wood for Trustle-trees, both our Main and Fore being broke; but the Weather was so

Wet and violent Sultry, that we could do nothing. Here are abundant Graves of Dead Men; and the Portugees told us that two great French ships, homeward bound from the South Seas, that Watered in this same place about nine months before, had buried nearly Half their men here; but 'twas at the Sickly season, and the French have a marvellous foul way of Living. The people very Civil; and we offered 'em handsome Gratuities if they would catch such of our men as might run away, which they promised to do most Cheerfully.

Hearing of a Brigantine (this was some days afterwards) at the entrance of the Bay of Grande, we sent our Pinnace manned and armed to know all about her. She turned out to be a Portugee laden with Negroes, poor Creatures! for the Gold-mines. Our boat returned, and brought as presents a Roove of Fine Sugar and a Pot of Sweetmeats from the Master, who spoke a little English, and had formerly sailed with 'em. The Portugees are cautious in saying how far it is to the Gold-mines; but, I believe, the distance by water is not great;

and there is certainly abundance of Gold in
the country.   The French took about 1200*l.*
worth out of their boats last autumn at one
Haul, which makes the Portugees hate 'em
so.   Some of 'em brought us a Monstrous
Creature which they had killed, having
Prickles or Quills like a Hedgehog, and the
head and tail of a Monkey.   It stank
abominably, which the Portugees said was
only the Skin, and that the Meat of it was
very Delicious, and often used for the table;
but our men not being yet on Short Commons, none of 'em had Stomach enough to
try the Experiment, so that we were forced
to throw it overboard to make a Sweet Ship.
Our people could now hardly go ashore
without being frightened, as they thought,
by Tigers, and holloaing to be taken aboard
again; but there was nothing more dangerous hereabouts than Apes and Baboons.

Twenty-seventh November was a grand
Festival at Angre de Keys, in honour of one
of their Saints.   We, and most of our
officers from the *Hope* and the *Delight*, went
ashore and were received by the Governor,

Signor Raphael da Silva Lagos, with much civility. He asked if we would see the Convent and Procession; and on our telling him our Religion differed very much from his, answered that we were willing to see it without partaking in the Ceremony. We waited on him in a Body, being ten of us, with two Trumpets and Hautboys, which he desired might play us to Church, where our Music did the office of an Organ, but separate from the Singing, which was very well chanted by the Padres. Our Trumpets and Hautboys played " Hey Boys, up go we!" and all manner of paltry noisy tunes; and, after service, the Musicians, who were by this time more than half-drunk, marched at the head of the Company : next to them an old Padre and two Friars, carrying Lamps of Incense. Then the Image of the Saint, as Fine as a Milkmaid's Garland, borne on a Bier, all spangled, on the shoulders of four men, and bedizened out with Flowers, Wax-candles, &c. After these, the Padre Guardian of the Convent, and about forty Priests in their full Habits.

Next came the Governor; Captain Blokes, in a blue Navy Coat laced with Gold, a pair of scarlet-velvet Breeches, and a Military Hat; and the rest of the English officers in their very best Apparel. I was fit to die a-laughing, and whispered to our Doctor of Physic, that had I known I was fated to walk in such a Procession, I would never have sold my old Tower Warder's slashed doublet to the Frippery Man in Monmouth Street, but would have brought it round the World with me to wear at this Outlandish place. Each of us had, moreover, in Compliment to his Saintship, a long Candle, lighted, in his hand; the which gave us great Diversion, flaring the tapers about, and seeking to smoke one another. The Ceremony held about two hours, after which we were splendidly entertained at the Convent, and then by the Governor at the Guard-house, his own habitation being about three leagues off. It is to be noted, they Kneeled at every Crossway, and turning, walked round the Convent, and came in at another door, bowing down and paying their devotion to the Images and the Wax-candles, with the like superstitious obser-vances. They unanimously told us, how-ever, that they expected nothing from us but our Company; and, beyond the Trum-pets and Hautboys, and a jolly Song or two from us, they had no more. Many Sharks were in the Road, that keep the Negro Slaves in good order, should they, poor Black Fellows, attempt Escape to any foreign ship by swimming to her. But the Portugees are not very hard with their Negroes, save up at the Gold-mines, where Mercy is quite unknown. *Aqua d'oro* may be a very good Eye-water; but, sure, there's nothing like it for hardening of the Heart.

On the 28th of this Month we bade fare-well to our kind friends of Angre de Keys. Just before sailing we sent a Boat to the town for more Necessaries, and brought off some Gentlemen, whom we treated to the very best we could. They were very glori-ous, and in their Cups proposed the Pope's Health to us; but we were quits with 'em by toasting that of the Archbishop of Canterbury; and, to keep up the humour, we also proposed Martin Luther: but this fell flat, as they had never Heard of him; whereas that of his Grace at Lambeth turned out rather against us than for us; for they cried out that they knew him very well, and that he was a Catholic Saint, under the style and title of San Tomaso de Cantorberi.

December 1st, we weighed with a breeze at N.E.; but later came on a gale S.S.W., forcing us to anchor close under the Island of Grande. About 10 next morning we weighed again, and bore away and steered away S.W. Now the product of Brazil is well known to be Red Wood, Sugars, Gold, Tobaccos (of every kind, and very choice), Whale Oil, Snuff, and several sorts of Drugs. The Portugees build their best ships here. The people very Martial; and 'tis but a few years since they would be under no Government, but have now submitted to the House of Braganza, which makes a Pretty Penny out of them. Their Customs are very nasty; their Houses mar-

vellously foul; and they are for ever smoking of Tobacco; but the Portugees are still
a very friendly folk, cordial to us English,
although they call us Heretics, and, but for
their great love for roasting Jews, very
tender-hearted. I like them much better
than those Proud Paupers the Spaniards.
A Beggar on Horseback is bad enough; but
Goodness deliver us from a Beggar on an
Andalusian Jackass!

Memorandum.——Brazil discovered by the
famous Americus Vespucius, that came after
Captain Christopher Colomb.

Nothing remarkable happened until December 6th, when we had close cloudy
Weather, with Showers; and, after that,
some pretty sharp Gales. On the 15th the
colour of the water changed; and we
sounded, but had no ground. On the 18th
one of the *Hope's* men fell out of the Mizen-
top on the Quarter-deck, and broke his
Skull; so that he died, and was buried next
day. A brisk fellow, that, from his merry
ways, used to be called Brimstone Jemmy.
After this, cold airy weather, and numbers

of Porpoises, black on their backs and fins, with sharp white Noses. They often leaped high up in the water, showing their white bellies. Also, a plenty of seals. December 23d we saw Land, appearing first in three, and afterwards in several Islands. The Wind being westerly, and blowing fresh, we could not weather it, but were forced to bear away and run along Shore from three to four leagues distant. This we saw first was Falkland's Land, described in few Draughts, and none lay it down right, though the Latitude agrees pretty well. December 25th saw Land again; but could not get near enough to see whether it was inhabited; in truth we were too much in a hurry to think of making Discoveries; for at four in the Afternoon we sighted a Sail under our Lee-bow, gave chase, and got ground of her apace till Night came on. In the Morning we saw nothing, it being thick hazy Weather; then, as ill luck would have it, it fell Calm, and having nothing else to do we Piped all hands to Punishment, and gave the Cook three dozen for burning Captain

Blokes' burgoo. Then Grog served out, and we took an Observation. Lat. 52·40.

We kept on rowing and towing with Sweeps, and our Boats ahead, until about six in the Evening; and the Chase appearing to be a large ship, we sent Boats aboard our Consorts, and agreed to engage her. A fine breeze sprang up, and we got in our Sweeps and Boats, making all possible sail; it came on thick again; but we kept her open on the Larboard, and the *Hope* and *Delight* on the Starboard bow, and it being now Short Nights, we thought it impossible to lose one another. But the Master persuaded our Commander to shorten sail, saying that we should lose our Consorts if we kept on. Another Fog, and be hanged to it; but the next morning the Yellow Curtain was lifted up, and we saw the Chase about four miles ahead, which gave us a new Life. We ran at a great Rate, it being smooth water; but it coming on to blow more and more, the Chase outbore our Consorts, and being to windward she gave off, and then came down very melancholy to us,

supposing her to be a French Homeward-
bound Ship from the South Seas. Thus,
this Ship escaped; and left us all, from the
Commander to the Cabin-boys (who had a
hard time of it that night, you may be sure),
in the most doleful Dumps.

Strong gales to the 1st of January. This
being New-Year's Day, every officer was
wished a Merry New Year by our Trumpets
and Hautboys; and we had a large tub of
Punch, hot, upon the Quarter-deck, where
every man in the Ship had above a Pint to
his share, and drank to our Owners' and
Friends' healths in Great Britain, to a Happy
New Year, a good Voyage, plenty of Plunder (Wo is me for that Homeward-bound
Frenchman from the Southern Seas!), and
a Safe Return. And then we bore down
on our Consorts and gave them three Huzzas,
wishing them the like.

Now, it being very raw cold Weather, we
very much dreaded scudding upon Ice; so
we fired Guns as Signals for the *Hope* and
Delight to bring to, and on the 5th of January brought ourselves to, under the same

reefed Topsails.   We feared at one time,
from our Consorts having an Ensign in
their Maintopmast shrouds, as a Signal of
Distress, that they had sprung their Mainmast; so we made the Large again, our
Ship working very well in a mighty great
sea.   When we were able to get within
Hail of our Consorts, we asked them how
they did, and how they had come to hoist
the Wretched Rag. They answered, Pretty
well, but that they had shipped a great deal
of Water in lying by, and being forced to
put before the wind, the Sea had broke in
at the Cabin Windows, filling the Steerage
and Waist, and was like to have spoiled
several Men; but, Heaven be thanked! all
else was indifferent well with 'em; only it
was intolerably Cold, and everything Wet.
Captain Blokes sent me on board the *Delight* in our Yall, and I found them in a
very disorderly Pickle, with all their Clothes
a-drying: the Ship and Rigging covered
with 'em from the Deck to the Maintop.
They got six of their Guns into the Hold,
to make the Ship lively.

Aboard the *Marquis* died, on the 8th, John Veale, a Landsman, having lain ill a Fortnight, and had a Swelling in the Legs ever since he left the Island of Grande. At nine at night we buried him; and this was the first we had lost by Sickness since we left England. Until the 15th, cloudy Weather with Squalls of Rain, and fresh Gales at S.W. We now accounted ourselves round Cape Horn, and so in the South Seas. The French ships that first came to trade in these seas were wont to come through the Straits of Magellan; but Experience has taught 'em since, that this is the best Passage to go round the Horn, where they have Sea Room enow, without being crushed and crowded as at a Ranelagh Masquerade; and the Straits are in many places very narrow, with strong Tides and no Anchor Ground.

On the 31st of January, at seven in the Morning, we made the Island of Juan Fernandez, bearing W.S.W., and about two in the Afternoon we hoisted our Pinnace out, and essayed to send one of our Lieutenants ashore, though we could not be less than four leagues off. As soon as it was Dark our men cried out that they saw a Light ashore; our Boat was then about a mile from the Shore, and bore away for the Ship on our firing a Quarter-deck Gun, and several Muskets, showing Lanterns in our Mizen and Foreshrouds, that the Pinnace might find us again, whilst we plied to the lee of the Island. About two in the Morning she came aboard, all safe. Next day we sent our Yall ashore about noon with the Master and Six Men, all well Armed; meanwhile we cleared all ready for Action on board the *Marquis.* Our Boat did not return, so we sent our Pinnace with the Crew, likewise Armed: for we were afraid that the Spaniards might have had a Garrison there, and so seized 'em. However, the Pinnace returned, and brought abundance of Crawfish, but found nothing human; so that the alarm about the Light must have been a mere superstition of the Ship's Company.

It was at this same Island of Juan Fernandez, in the year of our Lord 1708-9, *that*

Captain Woodes Rogers, commanding the " Duke " Frigate, and with whom also Captain Dampier, that famous Circumnavigator, sailed, found a Man clothed in Goatskins, who looked wilder than they who had been the first owners of 'em. He had been on the Island four years and four months, being left there by Captain Stradling in the " Cinque Ports ;" his name was ALEXANDER SELKIRK, a Scottish man, who had been Sailing Master to the " Cinque Ports ;" but quarrelling with the Commander, was by him accused of Mutiny, and so Abandoned on this Uninhabited Island. During his stay he saw several Ships pass by, but only two came to an Anchor. As he went to view 'em he found they were Spaniards, and so retired, upon which they Shot at him. Had they been French, he would have submitted ; but chose to risk his dying alone on the Island rather than fall into the hands of the Spaniards, because he apprehended they would Murder him, or make a Slave of him in the Mines ; for he feared they would spare no Stranger that might be capable of Discovering the South

Sea. He had with him when left his Clothes and Bedding, with a Firelock, some Powder, Bullets, and Tobacco, a Hatchet, a Knife, a Kettle, a Bible, some practical Pieces, and some Mathematical Instruments and Books. During the first eight months of his stay he suffered much from Melancholy and Terror; but afterwards got on pretty well. He built two Huts with Pimento Wood, which he also burnt for Fuel and Candle; and which, besides, refreshed him with its fragrant smell. He had grown very Pious in his Retreat, and was much given to singing of Psalms, having before led a very naughty life. Being a very good sailor, Captain Woodes Rogers took him away with him as Second Mate. He told 'em that he had been at first much pestered with Cats and Rats, the latter of which gnawed his feet and clothes, so that he was obliged to cherish the Cats with Goat's-flesh, and they grew so familiar with him as to lie about him in hundreds. But I cannot stay to recount half the wonderful Adventures of Mr. Selkirk. I knew him afterwards, a very old Man, lodging with one Mrs. Branbody, that kept a

Chandler's Shop over against the Jews' Harp Tavern at Stepney.   He was wont bitterly to complain that the Manuscript in which he had written down an Account of his Life at Juan Fernandez had been cozened out of him by some crafty Booksellers ; and that a Paraphrase, or rather Burlesque, of it, in a most garbled and mutilated form, had been printed as a Children's Story-book, under the name of ROBINSON CRUSOE. *This was done by one Mr. Daniel Foe, a Newswriter, who, in my Youth, stood in the Pillory by Temple Bar, for a sedition in some plaguey Church-matters.   But it is fitting to let these Gentry know that they have Ears, lest they become too Saucy.*

CHAPTER THE THIRD.

THE CONTINUATION OF MY VOYAGE UNTIL MY RETURN AGAIN TO EUROPE.

Now, being got away from Juan Fernandez, did an unconquerable Greed and Longing for Prize and Plunder come over us; and did we sweep the Horizon hour after hour as long as it was Light, in hope of satisfaction to our long-deferred Hope. March 2d we sighted Land, and a vast high ridge of Mountains they call the Cordilleras, and are in the Country of Chili. Some parts are, I believe, full as high, if not higher, than the Pico of Teneriffe, and the tops of all of 'em covered with Snow. This day we came to an allowance of Three Pints of Water a day for each man; judging it best to be Economical, although we had a good stock of water aboard (taken in at Juan Fernandez); but Captain Blokes' reason was, to be able to keep at Sea for some time longer, and take some Prizes to keep the Deuce out of our pockets, without being discovered by Watering; for our South-Sea Pilot told us that the timorous people of these Latitudes once smelling an Enemy hovering about, will put to sea with nothing of value from one end of the Coast to the other.   Much baffled by several white Rocks that looked like Ships, and Captain Blokes much incensed at continual Disappointments, takes to making the Cabin-boy weary of his life; and after drubbing him with a Rope's end three times doubled, was for sousing him in the Pickle-tub; but I dissuaded him (remembering the Torments I had myself endured as a Moose; and even now when I think of 'em I am Afraid, and Trembling takes hold of my Flesh), and so no more was Done to him, beyond a Threat that he should be Keel-hauled next time; although the poor lad had in no way misbehaved himself.   We got the two Pinnaces into the water, to try 'em under sail, having fixed each of 'em with a Gun, after the manner of a Patterero, to be useful as small Privateers, hoping they'd be serviceable to us in little winds to take vessels. March 15th, Land again, and we supposed it was Lobos; and sure enough, on the 17th, we got well unto anchor off that Island, but found nobody at the place. On the 19th we determined to fit out our small Bark for a Privateer, and launched her into blue water, under the name of the *Beginning.* To his great pride and delight, Captain Blokes appointed the Doctor of Physic to command her. She was well built for sailing, so she was had round to a small Cove in the Southernmost part of Lobos. A small Spar out of the *Marquis* made a Mainmast for her, and one of our Mizen Topsails was altered to make her a Mainsail. March 21st, All being ready, and the *Beginning* christened by Captain Blokes emptying a Bowl of hot Punch over her bow, she was victualled from the general store; and the Doctor of Physic, who, for all his Degree, claimed to be a good Mariner, took possession of his high and important command.   Twenty men from our ship, and ten from our Consorts, were put aboard her, all well Armed.   We saw her out of the Harbour, and she looked very pretty, having all Masts, Sails, Rigging, and Materials, like one of those Half Galleys fitted out for his Majesty's Service in England.   They gave our Ship's Company three Huzzas, and we returned them the like at parting.   We told the Captain-Doctor that if we were forced out of the Road, or gave chase hence, we would leave a Glass Bottle, buried under a remarkable Great Stone agreed upon, with Letters in it, to give an Account of how it was with us at the moment of our Departure, and where to meet again.   And he was to do the like.   When the *Beginning* was gone we fell to and scrubbed Ship, getting abundance of Barnacles off her much bigger than Mussels.   Seals numerous, but not so many as at Juan Fernandez.   A large one seized upon a fat Dutchman that belonged to us, and had like to have pulled him into the water, biting him to the bone about the arms and legs. This Hollander was henceforth known as the Lord Chancellor, having been so very near the Great Seal. After barnacling, we gave the *Marquis* a good Keel, and Tallowed her low down. Another Dutchman we had died of the Scurvy. His Messmates said that it was because we had no more Cheese aboard, and that we could not catch Red Herrings by angling for them in Blue Water.

March 28th. The little *Beginning* came in with a Prize, called the *Santa Josepha*, bound from Guayaquil to Truxillo, 50 tons burden, full of Timber, with some Cocoanuts and Tobacco. A very paltry Spoil. There were about twelve Spaniards aboard, who told us (after some little Persuasion, in the way of Drubbing) that the Widow of the late Viceroy of Peru would shortly embark at Acapulco, with her Family and Riches, and stop at Payta to Refresh; and that about eight months ago there was a Galleon with 200,000 pieces of Eight on board, that passed Payta on her way to Acapulco. They continued, however, to

Lie and Contradict themselves when questioned; and so (as they howled most dismally on deck while under Punishment) they were had down to the Cockpit, where the Boatswain and his Mates had their Will of them, and I don't know what became of them afterwards. These Spanish Prisoners give a great deal of Trouble.

April 2d. The Superstitious among us were heartily frightened at the Colour of the Water, which for several miles looked as Red as any Blood. Some fellows among the crew that were of a Preaching Turn, gave out that this unusual appearance was an Omen, or Warning to us of Judgments coming for what had been done to the Spanish Prisoners (in the which Duresse I declare I had no hand; 'twas all done by Captain Blokes' orders, and 'tis very likely that the Boatswain, who was a Rough Fellow, very ignorant, exceeded his instructions). It was explained, however, that this Sanguinary Hue in the water was a perfectly natural appearance, caused by the Spawn of Fish; and two or three of the preaching fellows being had to the Maingears and well Drubbed, Grog was served out to the rest, and an Alarm, which might have bred a Mutiny, soon subsided.

But huzza! on the 5th of April we had things more substantial to think of than Red Seawater; for we took, after a very slight Resistance, a Ship called the *Ascension,* built Galleon-fashion, very high, with Galleries, Burden between 400 and 500 tons, and two Brothers Commanders, both Dons of families that were Grandees 500 years before Adam was born, and of course with five-and-twenty Christian Names apiece. She had a number of Passengers and some fifty Negroes; but the former being persons of Condition, far above the Common Sort, and not poor Coasting people, such as were those in the Timber Bark, we used 'em handsomely. They, without any such persuasion as was employed to their forerunners, told us that the Bishop of Chokeaqua, a place far up the Country in the South Parts of Peru, was to have come from Panama in this vessel for Lima, but would stop at

Payta to Recruit.   Being near that' place, we resolved to Watch narrowly, in order to catch his Lordship.

Now to the Norrard, and on the 10th of April we were off the Hummocks they call the Saddle of Payta; and being very Calm, we held a Court-Martial on one of our Midshipmen who had threatened to shoot one of our men when at Lobos, merely for refusing to carry some Crows that he had shot.   The Court was held in Captain Blokes' Cabin, and consisted of the Commander, Self, First-Lieutenant, assisted in our deliberations by sundry Pipes of Tobacco and a great Jug of Punch.   Found Guilty. Sentenced to be Degraded before the Mast, to have his Grog stopped for a Fortnight, and to receive Four Dozen at the Gun (for he being a kind of Officer, we did not wish to Humiliate him on deck).   Half of his Punishment he endured with more doleful Squalling than ever I heard from a Penitent in my Life, although the Boatswain was very tender with him, and three Tails of the Cat were tied up.   He begged pardon, and so Captain Blokes remitted him the rest of his Punishment. This Midshipman was one who sang a very good Song; and so a Cushion being brought to Ease him, we finished the Evening and the Punch jovially enough, he being before the end in high favour with the Commander, and promised his Rating back again.

April 15th. The Officers of all three Ships met on board the *Marquis*, and the Committee came to a Resolution to attack Guayaquil at once. The Bark we had called the *Beginning* by this time had come back to us, having begun nothing and found nothing, since its first prize, except a great Sea Lubber, some kind of Monster that the Doctor of Physic had caught and wanted to preserve in Rum, to make a Present of to the Royal Society when we came Home; but we forbade his wasting good Liquor for so unworthy an end, and the Monster, smelling intolerably, was thrown overboard. 'Twould have caused me no great sorrow to see the Doctor follow his Prodigy, for he was a very uncomfortable

Person, and was much given to cheating at Cards.

April 20th. To our Boats off Guayaquil, a Great Company of Men and Officers all armed to the teeth. We rowed till 12 at night, when we saw Lights, which we judged to be a place called Puna. It blew fresh, with a small rolling Sea, the Boat I commanded being deep laden and crammed with men; some of us say they would rather be in a Storm at Sea than here; but, in regard we were about a charming Undertaking, we thought no Fatigue too hard. At daybreak we saw a Bark above us in the River; and, running down upon her, found it was a large Pinnace, full of the most considerable Inhabitants of Puna, escaping towards Guayaquil. Here were at least a dozen handsome genteel young Women, extremely well dressed, and from them our men got some fine Gold Chains and Earrings. Some of these Nicknacks were concealed about 'em; but the Gentlewomen in these parts being very thinly dressed in Silk and Fine Linen, they could hide but little, and our

Linguist was bidden to advise them to be Wise in Time, and surrender their Valuables, which they did. And so civil were our Sailors to them, that they offered to dress some Victuals for us when we got 'em aboard; which made us hope that the Fair Sex would be kind to us when we returned to England, for our discreet behaviour to these charming Prisoners.

*　　*　　*　　*　　*

I am afraid that during the Attack on Guayaquil, which took place the next day, and continued for the three following ones, when the place Capitulated to our force, and a Treaty was signed between our Commanders and the Governor and Corregidor of Guayaquil, sundry proceedings took place that would not very well have squared with the public ideas of what is due to the Fair Sex just treated of; but I declare that I had neither Art nor Part in them, and that I am entirely Free from any Responsibility that Censure might cast on the Authors of Cruel Disturbances; for early in the Attack I was hit by a Musket-ball in the chest, and borne

senseless to our Boats.   That I did my Duty
bravely, my Commander was good enough
to say, and the whole Ship's Company to
admit.   I was carried away to the *Marquis*,
and for a long time lay between Hawk and
Buzzard; for a smart Fever came about the
third day, like Burgundy wine after Sherris,
and I was for awhile quite off my head and
Raving about Old Times;—about Captain
Night and the Blacks, and Maum Buckey
and her Negro Washerwomen, and my
Campaign against the Maroons, and some
Other Things that had befallen me during
those fifteen years which I have chosen to
leave a Blank in my life, and which I scorn
to deny did—some of them—lie heavy on
my Conscience.   All these were mixed up
with the old Gentleman at Gnawbit's, and
my Lord Lovat with his head off, and my
Grandmother in Hanover Square; so that I
doubt whether those who tended me knew
what to make of me.   There was some difficulty too as to medical attendance, for we
had cashiered our Surgeon—that is to say,

he had run away at Grande in the Brazils, to marry a brown Portugee woman; and the Doctor of Physic he was all for Herbal Treatment, demanding Succory, Agrimony, Asarabacca, Knights-pound-wort, Cuckoo-point, Hulver-bush, with Alehoof, and other things not to be found in this part of the World. And Captain Blokes said that he knew nothing half so good for a Gunshot Wound as cold Rum-and-Water; and between the two I had like to have died, but all were very kind to me, even to extracting the Ball with a Pair of Snuffers; and a great clumsy thing the said missile was, being, I verily believe, part of a Door-hinge which these clumsy Spanish Brutes had broken off short to cram into their Guns; and yet it might have gone worse with me had it been a smooth round cast Bullet, and drilled a clean Wound right through my Body.

As I was coming round, even to the taking of some Sangaree and Chicken Panada (for we were now very well provided with Live Stock), the Captain said to me: "You ha'n't murdered a man, Brother, have you?"

I replied, starting up, that my hands were free from the stain of Bood unrighteously spilt.

"No offence, Brother Dangerous," continued the Captain. "In our line of life we ar'n't particular. It wouldn't take very dirty weather to make our Ensign look like a Black Flag. Piracy and Privateering— they both begin with a P. I thought you had something o' that sort on your mind, because you took it so woundily about being hanged."

"I have had a strange life," I answered faintly.

"No doubt about that," says the Captain. "So have I, Brother, and not an overgood one: that's why I asked you. If the old woman hadn't been in the oven herself, she'd never have gone there to look for her daughter. But have you anything on your mind, Brother? Is there anything that Billy Blokes can do for you?"

I answered, very gratefully, that there was nothing I could think of.

"'Cause why," he resumed, "if there is, you have only to sing out. If you think you're like to slip your Cable and would like to say something, we've got a Padre on board out of the last Prize, and he shall come and do the Right Thing for you. You don't know anything about his lingo; but what odds is that? Spanish, or Thieves' Latin, or rightdown Cockney, — it's all one when the word's given to pipe all hands."

I answered that I was no Papist, but a humble member of the Church of England as by Law established.

"Of course," concluded the Captain. "So am I. God bless King George and the Protestant Succession, and confound the Pope, the Devil, and the Pretender! But any Port in a storm, you know; and a Padre's better than no Prayers at all. I've done all I could for you, Brother. I've read you most part of the story of Bel and the Dragon, likewise the Articles of War, and a lot of psalms out of Sternhold and Hopkins; and now, if you feel skeery about losing the number of your mess, I'll make your Will for you, to be all shipshape before the Big Wigs of London. There must be a matter of Four Hundred Pounds coming to you already for your share of Plunder; and no one shall say that Billy Blokes ever robbed a Messmate of even a twopenny tester of his Rights."

Again I thanked this singular person, who, for all his Addictedness to Rum-and-Water, of which he drank vast quantities, was one of the most Sagacious men I have known. But I told him that I had neither kith nor kin belonging to me; that I did not even know the name of my Father and Mother; and that my Grandmother, even, was an Unknown Lady, and been dead nigh forty years. Finally, that if I made my Will, it would only be to the effect that my Property, if any, might be divided among the Ship's Company of the *Marquis*, with a donative of Fifty guineas to the *Hope* and *Delight* people to drink to my Memory.

"Ay, and to a pleasant journey to Fiddler's Green," cries out the Captain. " But cheer up, Heart; ye're not weighed for the Long Journey yet." Nor had I; for I presently recovered, and in less than a month after my Mishap was again whole and fit for Duty. And I have set this down in order to confute those malignant men who have declared that all my Wounds were from Stripes between the Shoulders; whereas I can show the marks, 1°, of an English Grenadier's bayonet; 2°, of a Frenchman's sword; 3°, of a Spanish bullet; with many more Scars gotten as honourably, and which it would be only braggadocio to tell the History of.

Item.—The Corregidores, or Head-Men of Guayaquil, are great Thieves. The Mercenary Viceroys not being permitted to Trade themselves, do use the Corregidores as middle-men, and these again employ a third hand; so that ships are constantly employed carrying Quicksilver, and all manner of precious and prohibited goods, to and from Mexico out of by-ports. Thus, too, being their own Judges, they get vast Estates, and stop all complaints in Old Spain by Bribes. But now and then comes out a Viceroy who is a Man of Honesty and Probity, and will have none of these Scoundrelly ways of Making Money (like Mr. Henry Fielding among the Trading Justices, a Bright exception for integrity, though his Life, as I have heard, was otherwise dissolute), and then he falls too and squeezes the Corregidores, in the same manner as Cardinal Richelieu, that was Lewis Thirteenth's Minister, was wont to do with the Financiers. " You must treat 'em like Leeches," said he; " and when they are bloated with blood, put salt upon them, to make them disgorge." And I have heard that this rigid System of Probity, and putting salt on the gorged Corregidores, has ofttimes turned out more profitable to the Viceroys than trading on their own account.

Many of our men falling sick here, and our Ransom being now fully disbursed by the authorities of Guayaquil, we made haste to get away from the place, which was fast becoming pestiferous.

We set sail with more than fifty men Down with the Distemper (of which they were dying like Sheep with the Rot in the town, and all the Churches turned into Hospitals); but we hoped the Sea Air, for which we longed, would set us all healthy again. So plying to windward, bearing for the Galligapos Islands, and on the 21st of May made the most Norrard of that Group. Jan Serouder, a West Frieslander, and very good Sailor, though much given to smoking in his Hammock, for which he had many times been Drubbed, died of the Distemper. A great want of Medicines aboard, and the Rum running very low. Sent a boat ashore to see for Water, Fish, and Turtle, which our men (being now less Dainty by Roughing) had, by this time, condescended to eat. Kept on our course; on the 27th the Easternmost Island bore S.E. by S., distant about four leagues: and nothing more re-markable happened till the 6th of June, when we spied a Sail, the *Hope* being then about two miles ahead of us; and about seven in the Evening she took her in a very courageous manner. This was a Vessel of about 90 tons, bound from Panama to Guayaquil, called the *San Tomaso y San Demas* (for these Spaniards can never have too much of a good thing in the way of Saints), Juan Navarro Navarret y Colza, Commander. About forty people on board, and eleven Negro Slaves, but little in the way of European goods save some Iron and Cloth. They had a passenger of note on board, one Don Pantaleone and Something as long as my Arm, who was going to be Governor of Baldivia, and said he had been taken not long since in the North Sea by Jamaica Cruisers. On the 7th June we made the Island of Gorgona; and, on the 8th, got to an anchor in 30-fathom water. The next day sent out our Pinnace a'cruis-ing, and took a prize called the *Golden Sun*, belonging to a Creek on the Main, — a twopenny-halfpenny little thing, 35 tons; ten Spaniards and Indians, and a Negro that was chained down to the deck to amuse the Ship Company with playing on the Guitar (a kind of Lute). However, we found a few ounces of Gold-dust aboard her, worth some sixty pounds sterling. After examining our Prisoners (who gave us much trouble, for we had no Linguist, and 'twas a Word and a Blow in questioning them: that is, the Blow came from us to get the Word from 'em; but not more than two or three Spaniards were Expended),—after this tedious work was over we held a Committee, and agreed to go to Malaga,* an Island which had a Road, and with our Boats tow up the River in quest of the rich Gold-mines of Barbacore, also called by the Spaniards San Juan. But heavy Rains coming on, we were obliged to beat back and come to Gorgona again, building a Tent ashore for our Armour and Sick Men. We

---

* There is a River in Macedon and a River in Monmouth, and more Malagas than one.

spent till the 25th in Careening; on the 28th we got all aboard agen, rigged and stowed all ready for sea; the Spaniards who were our Prisoners, and who are very Dilatory Sailors (for they hearken more to their Saints than to the Boatswain's Pipe), were much amazed at our Despatch; telling us that they usually took Six Weeks or a Month to Careen one of their King's Ships at Lima, where they are well provided with all Necessaries, and account that Quick Expedition. We allowed Liberty of Conscience on board our floating Commonwealth to our Prisoners; for there being a Priest in each ship, they had the Great Cabin for their Mass, whilst we used the Church-of-England Service over them on the Quarter-deck. So that the Papists here were the Low Churchmen. Shortly after the beginning of July we freed our prisoners at fair Ransom in Gold-dust; but the Village where we landed them was so poor in common Necessaries, that we were obliged to give them some corned beef and biscuit for their subsistence until they could get up the Country, where there was a Town. Same day a Negro belonging to the *Delight* was bit by a small brown speckled Snake, and died in a few hours.

We had with us, too, a very good prize taken by the *Hope*, and continued unloading this and transferring the rich contents to our ships, having promised to restore the Hull itself to the Spaniards, on her being handsomely Ransomed; and the Don that was to be Governor of Baldivia was appointed Agent for us, and suffered to go freely on his Parole to and fro to arrange Money-Matters with the Authorities up the Country.

Memorandum.—Amongst our Prisoners (taken on board the Panama ship) there was a Gentlewoman and her Family, the Eldest Daughter, a pretty young woman of Eighteen, newly Married, and had her husband with her. We assigned them the Great Cabin on board the Prize, and none were suffered to intrude amongst them; yet the Husband (we were told) showed evident Marks of a Violent Jealousy, which is the Spaniard's Epidemic Disease. I hope he had not the least Reason for it, seeing that the Prize-Master (our Second Lieutenant) was above Fifty years of Age, and of a very Grave Countenance, appearing to be the most secure Guardian to females that had the least Charm, though all our young Men (that were Officers) had hitherto appeared Modest beyond Example among privateers; yet we thought it improper to expose them to Temptation. And I am sure, when the Lieutenant, being superseded for somewhat Scorching of a Negro with a stick of fire for answering him Saucily, and Captain Blokes bade me take temporary command of the Prize and Prisoners, that I behaved myself so well as to gain Thanks and Public Acknowledgments for my civility to the Ladies. We had notice that more than one of these Fair Creatures had concealed Treasure about 'em; and so in the most Delicate Manner we ordered a Female Negro who spoke English to overhaul 'em privately, and at the same time to tell 'em that it would pain us to the Heart to be obliged to use Stripes or other Unhandsome Means to come to a Discovery. Many Gold Chains, Bracelets, Ouches, and suchlike Whim-Whams the Sable Nymph found cunningly stowed away; upon which we gave her half a pint of Wine and a large pot of Sweets, forgiving her at the same time a Whipping at the Capstan which had been promised her for Romping and Gammocking among the people in the Forecastle. For I suppose there was never a modester man than Captain Blokes.

August 10th. All Money-Matters being arranged, we disposed of our Prisoners. We burnt down the Village for some Impertinence of the Head Man (who was a Half-caste Indian),—but no great harm done, since 'twas mostly Mud and Plantain thatch, and could be built up again in a Week,—and got to Windward very slowly, there being a constant current flowing to Leeward to the Bay of Panama. 13th we saw the Island of Gallo; the 18th we spied a Sail bearing W.N.W. of us, when we all three gave chase, and took her in half an hour. 70 tons. Panama to Lima. Forty people aboard, upon examining whom they could tell us little News from Europe, but said that there came Advices from Portobello in Spain, and by a French ship from France, not long before they came out of Panama; but that was all kept private; only, they heard that his Royal Highness the Duke of Cumberland was Dead, the which Sad Intelligence we were not willing to Believe, but drank his Health at Night, which we thought could do him no hurt even if he really happened to be Dead. By this time we had gotten another Surgeon out of the *Delight*, whom we daily exercised at his Instruments in the Cockpit, and his Mate at making of Bandages and spreading of Ointment; and Captain Blokes (who was always giving some fresh proof of Sagacity), just to try 'em, and imitate business for 'em a little, ordered Red Lead, mixed with Water, to be thrown on two of our Fellows, and sent 'em down to the Hold, when the Surgeon, thinking they had really been wounded, went about to Dress them; but the mistake being discovered, it was a very agreeable Diversion.

After this we made sail to the Marias Islands (for I feel I must be brief in this abstract of my Log, and must compress into a few pages the events of many Months), and all November were cruising about Cape St. Lucas in quest of Prizes. Christmas we spent in a very dismal manner; for a Complaint, something akin to Mumps with Scurvy in the gums, and a touch of Lockjaw to boot, broke out among us, and eight men died. Then we engaged or took a very big Spaniard out of Manilla, 250 tons, and a very rich Cargo, mostly in Gold-dust and embroidered Stuffs. January 10th, 1748-9, at anchor at Port Segura; and here, to our dismal dismay, we heard that Peace had been proclaimed between Spain and England, and that all our Privateering for the present was at an end. Then to Acapulco in Mexico, seeing if we could do some honest trading; but at all the Towns along the Coast they looked upon us as

little better than Pirates.   But we felt a
little comforted at the thought that we had
already taken some very rich Prizes, and
my own part of the Plunder was now over
1500*l*.   January 11th, we weighed from
Port Segura, and ran towards the Island
of Guam.   Our Steward missing some
pieces of Pork, we immediately searched
and found the Thieves.   One of them had
been guilty before, and Forgiven on promise of Amendment; but was punished
now, lest Forbearance should encourage
the rest to follow his bad practice.   Provisions being so short, and our run now so
long, might, without great caution, have
brought evil consequences upon us.   They
(the Thieves) were ordered to the Main-
gear, and every man of the watch to give
'em a blow with the Cat-o'-nine-tails.   On
the 14th of February, in commemoration
of the ancient English custom of choosing
Valentines, a list was drawn up of all the
Fair Ladies in Bristol in any way related
or concerned in our Ships; and all the
officers were sent for to the Cabin, where

every one drew, and drank his Valentine's health in a cup of Punch, and to a happy sight of 'em all. This was done to put 'em in mind of Home.

From Guam, a very poor place, and the Natives uncommonly nasty, we shaped our course to Ternate; and about the 2d of May saw land, which we took for some of the Islands lying about the N.E. part of Celebes, but were satisfied soon after that we were in the Straits of Guiana. 18th May passed several Islands, and the South point of Gillolo. This was the time of the S.E. Monsoon, which made Weather and Wind very uncertain. May 25th we fell in with a parcel of Islands to the Eastward of Bouton, an island where there is a kind of Indian King, very Savage and Warlike, and with a considerable flotilla of Galleys. We traded with him, and made good profit in the way of Barter; for these Savages will give gold and Goods for the veriest trumpery that was ever picked up at a Groat the handful at the hucksters' stalls in Barbican. From Bouton on the 11th June, having well watered and provisioned, and taken a Native pilot on board, we sailed for Batavia, and on the 30th cast anchor in the Road there. We waited on his Excellency the Governor-General (for the States of Holland), and begged permission to refit our Ships, which was granted. Many strange Humours now to be seen aboard. Some of the crew hugging each other; others blessing themselves that they were come to such a glorious place for Punch, where they could have Arrack for Eightpence a Gallon; for now the Labour was worth more than the Liquor, whereas, a few weeks since, a Bowl of Punch was worth more to them than half the Voyage. Now we began to Careen, going over to Horn Island, and a Sampan ready to heave down by, and take in our Guns, Carriages, &c. Several of our men fell ill of Fevers, as they said, from drinking the Water of the Island; but as Captain Blokes opined, more from the effects of Arrack Punch at Eightpence a Gallon. All English ships are allowed by the Government here half a leaguer of Arrack a day for ship's use per man; but boats are not suffered to bring the least thing off shore without being first severely searched. As to the town of Batavia, it lies in a bay full of islands, which so break off the Sea, that though the Road is very large, yet it is safe. The Banks of the Canals through the City are paved with stones as far as the Boom, which is shut up every night at nine o'clock, and guarded by Soldiers. All the Streets are very well built and inhabited; fifteen of 'em have Canals just as in Amsterdam and Rotterdam, and from end to end they reckon fifty-six bridges. The vast number of Cocoa-nut trees in and about the City everywhere afford delightful and profitable Groves. There are Hospitals, Spin-houses, and so forth, as in Holland, where the idle and vicious are set to work, and, when need arises, receive smart Discipline. The Chinese have also a large Sick House, and manage their charity so well that you never see a Chinaman looking despicable in the street. The Dutch Women have greater privileges in India than in Holland, or, indeed, anywhere else; for on slight occasions they are often divorced from their Husbands, and share the Estate betwixt 'em. A Lawyer told me at Batavia he had known, out of fifty-eight causes, all depending in the Council Chamber, fifty-two of them were Divorces. The Governor's Palace of Brick, very stately and well laid. He lives in as great splendour as a king; he has a Train and Guards—viz. a Troop of Horse and a Company of Foot with Halberds, in liveries of yellow satin adorned with silver laces and fringe—to attend his Coach when he goes abroad. His Lady has also her Guards and Train. The Javanese, or Ancient Natives, are numerous, and said to be barbarous and proud, of a dark colour, with flat faces, thin short Black hair, large eyebrows and cheeks. The Men are strong-limbed, but the Women small. The Men have many Wives, and are much given to lying and stealing. They are all Pagans, and worship Devils. The Women tawny, sprightly, and Amorous, and very apt to give poison to their Husbands when they can do it cunningly. There are at least 10,000

Chinese who pay the Dutch a dollar a month for liberty to wear their Hair, which they are not allowed to do at home since the Tartars conquered 'em. There comes hither from China fourteen or sixteen Junks a year, being flat-bottomed vessels. The Merchants come with their goods, and marvellous queer folks they are. I don't think the whole City is as large as Bristol; but 'tis much more populous.

October 12th. We, according to our Owners' orders to keep our Ships full-manned, whether the War continued or not —and, oh, how we cursed this plaguey Peace!—shipped here seventeen men that were Dutch. Though we looked upon our hardships as being now pretty well over, several Ran from us here that had come out of England with us, being straggling, lazy, good-for-nothings, that can't leave their old Trade of deserting, though now they had a good sum due to each of 'em for Wages. Their shares for Plunder of course were forfeited, and equitably divided among those that stuck by us. From this to the 23d we continued taking in wood and water for our Passage to the Cape of Good Hope; and just before we sailed held a Council on board the *Marquis*, by which 'twas agreed, that if any of our Consorts should happen to part company, the one that arrived first was to stay at the Cape twenty days; and, then, if they didn't find the other Ships, to make their utmost despatch to the Island of Helena; and if not there, to proceed, according to Owners' orders, to Great Britain.

Nothing particular happened till the 27th December, when the *Marquis* proved very Leaky, and rare work we had at the Pumps, they being most of them choked up from long disuse. December 28th we came in sight of the Lion's Head and Rump, being two Hills over the Cape Town. Saluted the Dutch fortress with Nine Guns, and got but Three for thanks; it being surprising what airs these Pipe-smoking, Herring-curing, Cheese-making, Twenty-breeches Gentry give themselves. 29th, we moored Ship, and sent our Sick ashore. We stayed here until the end of February, when we went into Sardinia Bay to Careen; for a Survey of Carpenters had reported very badly concerning the Leak. 27th Feb. we had a good rummage for Bale Goods to dispose of ashore, having leave of the Governor, and provided a Store-house, where I and the Supercargo of the *Delight* took it by turns weekly during the sale of 'em. 28th March came in a Portugee frigate, with news that Five stout French Ships had attempted Rio Janeiro, but were repulsed, and had a great number of men killed, with over 400 taken prisoners by the Portuguese.

April 5th we hoisted a Blue Ensign, loosened our Fore Topsail, and fired a Gun as a Signal for our Consorts to unmoor, and so fell down to Robin and Penguin Islands.

Memorandum.—We buried four while at the Cape; eight ran away to be eaten up, as we heartily hoped, by the Hottentots, who have a great gusto for White Man's Flesh; but reject Negroes as too strong and Aromatic; to say little of the major number of our Ship's Companies getting Married to

Black Wenches. But there's no Doctors' Commons at Cape Town; and the best Way of Divorce is by shoving off a boat from Shore, and leaving your Wife behind you. *Item.*—The Dutch generally send a Ship every year to Madagascar for Slaves to supply their Plantations; for the said beastly Hottentots have their Liberty and Ease so much, that they cannot be brought to work, even though they should Starve (which they do pretty well all the year round) for the lack of it. Here, too, we spoke with an Englishman and an Irishman, that had been several years with the famous Madagascar Pirates, but were now pardoned, and allowed to settle here. They told us that these Miserable Wretches, who once made such a Noise in the World, dwindled away one by one, most of them very poor and despicable, even to the Natives, among whom they had Married. They added, that they had no Embarkations, only mere Canoes and Rowboats in Madagascar; so that these Pirates (so long a terrible Bugbear to peaceable Merchantmen) are now become so inconsiderable as to be scarcely worth mentioning; yet I do think that if care be not always taken after a Peace to clear all out-of-the-way Islands of these piratical Vermin, and hinder others from joining them, it may prove a Temptation for loose scampish Fellows to resort thither, and make every Creek in the Southern Seas a troublesome nest of Freebooters.

The Cape having been so frequently described, I shall only add that the Character of the Hottentots, at which I have hinted, has been found to be too True, that they scarce deserve to be reckoned of the Human Kind: they are such a nasty, ill-looking, and worse-smelling people. Their Apparel is the Skins of Beasts; their chief Ornament is to be very Greasy and Black; so that they besmear themselves with an abominable Oil, mixed with Tallow and Soot; and the Women twist the Entrails of Beasts or Thongs of Hides round their legs, which resemble Rolls of Tobacco. Here's plenty, however, of all kinds of Flesh and Fowl;

there's nothing wanting at the Cape of Good Hope for a good subsistence; nor is there any place more Commodious for a Retirement to such as would be out of the Noise of the World, than the adjacent country in the possession of the Dutch.

Nothing of note happened till May 1st, only that sometimes we had Thunder, Lightning, Rain, and Squalls of Wind. On the 7th we made the Island of Ascension, S. Lat. 8.2. On the 14th at noon we found we had just crossed the Equator, being the eighth time we had done so in our course round the World. We had a Dutch Squadron with us, who expected Convoy Rates, and all manner of Civilities from us, though there was now Peace, and we wanted nothing from 'em; but 'tis always the way with this Grasping and Avaricious People. Soon too we observed that the Dutch ships began to scrape and clean their sides, painting and polishing and beeswaxing 'em inside and out, bending new sails, and the very Mariners putting on half a dozen pair of new breeches apiece. This it is their custom to do as they draw near home; so that they look as if newly come out of Holland.

On the morning of the 15th July we made Fair Island and Foul Island, lying off Shetland ; and sighted two or three Fishing Doggers cruising off the Islands. Having little wind, we lay by, and the Inhabitants came off with what Provisions they had; but they are very poor people, wild and savage, subsisting chiefly on Fish. When that provision fails, I have heard they live on Seaweed.

We being, so to speak, in charge, although unwillingly, of the Dutch Squadron, which had been willy-nilly our Convoy, were compelled to put into a port of Holland instead of into a British one, as we had fondly hoped. On the 23rd July the Dutch Commodore made a signal for seeing Land, and the whole fleet answered him with all their colours. The Pilot-boat coming off, we took two aboard, and about noon parted with some of our Dutch Consorts that were Rotterdam and Middleburg ships. We gave 'em a Huzza and a half in derision, and our

Trumpet and Hautboy were for striking up the Rogue's March; but this was forbidden by the Sagacious Captain Blokes. Some English ships now hove in sight, and saluted the Dutch Commodore; and afterwards we, though with an ill grace, saluted his Worship to welcome in sight of the land, which by right belongs to the Rats (though I have little doubt that for all the Vandykes and Vandams the long-whiskered Gentry will come to their own again some of these fine days). As soon as they got over the Bar the Dutchmen fired all their guns for joy at their safe arrival in their own country, which they very affectionately call Fatherland; and, indeed, it was not easy under these circumstances to be angry with the Poor Souls that had been so long at Sea, and wandering about Strange Lands. At 8 at night we came to an anchor in 6-fathom water, about 2 miles off shore.

On the 24th, in the morning, the Dutch Flag-ship weighed, in order to go up to the unlivering place. In the afternoon Captain Blokes sent me ashore, and up to Amsterdam, with a letter for our Owners' Agents, to ask how we were to act and proceed from hence. Coming back with instructions from the Agent (one Mr. Vandepeereboom, who made me half-fuddled with Schiedam drinking to our prosperous return; but he was a very Civil Gentleman, speaking English to admiration, and had a monstrous pretty Housekeeper, with eyes as bright as her own Pots and Pans), by Consent of our Council we discharged such men as we had shipped at Batavia and the Cape, and sold the half-dozen Negroes we had from time to time picked up for about a Hundred Dollars apiece. But this last had to be managed by private Contract, and somewhat under the Rose; for their High Mightinesses, the States-General, allow no Slaves to be sold openly in Amsterdam.

On the 10th we went up to the Vlieder, which is a better Road than the Texel, and then to Amsterdam again, where Captain Blokes and his chief officers had to make Affidavits before a Notary Public to the truth of an Abstract of our Voyage, the which I had drawn up from the Log of the *Marquis*, to justify our proceedings to our own Government in answer to what the East India Company had to allege against us; they being, as we were informed, resolved to trouble us on pretence that we had Encroached upon their Charter. On the 31st August comes Mr. Vandepeereboom on board to take Account of what Plate, Gold, and Pearl was in the Ship; and on the 5th September he took his leave of us.

But not of me; for as I had been much with him ever since we had lain at Amsterdam, we had become great Chums, and he had persuaded me not to return just yet to England, but to remain with him in Holland, and become his partner in Mercantile Adventure, that should not necessitate my going to Sea again. And by this time, to tell truth, I was heartily sick of being Tossed and Tumbled about by the Waves. No man could say that I had not done my Duty during my momentous Voyage round the World. I had worked as hard as any Moose on board the *Marquis*, doing hand-work and head-work as well. I had been Wounded, had had two Fevers and one bout of Scurvy; but was seldom in such evil case as to shirk either my Duty or my Grog. I prudently redoubted the Chances of returning in haste to my native Country, for, although being alone in the world, and the marriage with Madam Taffetas not provable in Law, with no other Domestic Troubles to grieve me, I knew from long experience what Ducks and Drakes Seafaring men do make of their money coming home from a long voyage with their heads empty and their pockets full, and was determined that what I had painfully gathered from the uttermost Ends of the Earth should not be riotously and unprofitably squandered in the Taverns of Wapping and Rotherhithe. Mr. Vandepeereboom entering with me into the State of his Affairs, proved, as far as Ledger and Cash-book could prove any thing, that he was in a most prosperous way of business, in the Dutch East India trade, of which by this time I knew something; so that, although Captain Blokes was loth to part with his old Shipmate and Secretary, he was yet glad to see me better myself. And in truth Mr. Vandepeereboom's Housekeeper was marvellous pretty. I drew my Pay and Allowances, which amounted to but a small matter; but to my great Joy and Gladness I found that my share of the Plunder from our Prizes and the Ransom of Guayaquil came to Twenty Hundred Pounds. The order for this sum was duly transferred to me, and lodged to my Account in the Bank of Amsterdam, then the most famous Corporation of Cofferers (since that of Venice began to decline) in Europe. I bade farewell to Captain Blokes and all my Messmates; left Twenty Pounds to be divided among the Ship's Company (for which they manned Shrouds and gave me three Huzzas as the Shoreboat put off); and after a last roaring Carouse on board the *Marquis*, gave up for Ever my berth in the gallant Craft in which I had sailed round the World.

CHAPTER THE FOURTH.

OF THE SINGULAR MISFORTUNES WHICH BEFELL ME IN HOLLAND.

'Twas no such very bad Title for a Mercantile Firm, " Vandepeereboom and Dangerous." Aha, Rogues! will you call me Pauper, Card-sharper, Led-Captain, Halfpenny-Jack, now ? Who but I was Mynheer Jan van Dangerous? (I took my Gentility out of my Trunk, as the Spanish Don did his Sword when the Sun shone and there were Pistoles galore, and added the Van as a prefix to which I was entitled by Lineage.) Who but I was a wealthy and prosperous Merchant of Amsterdam, the richest city in Holland? Soon was I well known and Capped to, as one that could order wine, and pay for it, at

the sign of the Amsterdam Wappen, the
great Inn here.

Although 'tis now nigh thirty years since,
I do preserve the pleasantest remembrance
of my life in the Low Countries; for, albeit
hating the Dutch when I was Poor, I grew
to like 'em as a reputable Merchant Adventurer. 'Twas but a small matter prevented me
from setting up my Coach, and was only
hindered by the fact that the Police Laws of
Amsterdam are very strict against Wheeled
carriages, allowing only a certain and very
small number, lest the rumbling of the
Wheels should disturb the good thrifty
Burghers at their Accompts. For most
vehicles they have what they call a Sley,
which is the body of a Coach fastened on to
a Sledge with ropes, and drawn by one
Horse. A Fellow walks by the side on't,
and holds on with one hand to prevent its
falling over, while with the other he ma-
nages the Reins. A most melancholy Machine this, moving at the rate of about
Three miles an hour, and makes you think
that you are in a Hospital Conveyance, or

else going on a Hurdle to be Hanged, Drawn, and Quartered.

This Amsterdam is the famous town built upon Wooden Piles, as is also Petersburg, and in some order Venice; and from its Timber supports, gave rise to the sportive saying of Erasmus when he first came hither, that he had reached a City where the Citizens lived, like Crows, upon the tops of Trees. And again he waggishly compared Amsterdam to a maimed Soldier, as having Wooden Legs. This Erasmus was, I conjecture, a kind of Schoolmaster, and very learned; but conceited, as are most Bookish Persons.

A Dutchman will save any thing; and this rich place has all come out of saving the Mud, and starving the Fishes. Here Traffic is wooed as though she were a Woman, and Gold is put to bed with Time, and there is much joy over their Bantling, which is christened Interest. A strange, cleanly, money-grubbing Country of Botanic Gardens and Spitting-pans, universal Industry and Tobacco-pipes, Gingerbread and

Sawing-mills, Tulip-roots and the Strong Waters of Schiedam, Cheese, Red Herrings, and the Protestant Religion. Peculiar to these People is the functionary called the Aansprecker, a kind of human Bird of Evil Omen, who goes about in a long Black Gown and a monstrous Cocked Hat with a Crape depending from it, to inform the Friends and Acquaintances of Genteel Persons of any one being Dead. This Aansprecker pays very handsome Compliments to the Departed, at so many Stuyvers the Ounce of Butter; and this saves the Dutch (who are very frugal towards their Dead) from telling lies upon their Tombstones. When a Man quits, they wind up his Accounts, strike a Balance, and go on to a fresh Folio in the Ledger without carrying any thing forward. At Marriage-time, also, is it the custom among Persons of Figure for the Bride and Bridegroom to send round Bottles of Wine, generally fine Hock, well spiced and sugared, and adorned with all sorts of Ribbons. They have also a singular mode of airing their Linen and Beds, by means of what they call a Trokenkorb, or Fire-basket, which is of the size and shape of a Magpie's Cage, and within it is a pan filled with burning Turf, and the Linen is spread over the Wicker-frame; or, to air the Bed, the whole Machine is placed between the Sheets. Nay, there are sundry Dowager Fraws who do warm their Legs with this same Trokenkorb, using it as though it were a footstool; and considering the quantity of Linsey Woolsey they wear, I wonder there are not more Fires. To guard against this last, there are Persons appointed whose office it is to remain all day and all night in the Steeples of the highest Churches; and as soon as they spy a Flame, they hang out a Flag if it's Day, or a Lantern if at Night, towards the quarter where the Fire is, blowing a Trumpet lustily meanwhile.

Eating and Drinking here very good, save the Water, which is so Brackish that it is not drunk even by the Common People. There are Water-Merchants constantly occupied in supplying the City with drinkable Water, which they bring in Boats from Utrecht and Germany in large stone Bottles, that cost you about Eightpence a-piece English. The Poor, who cannot afford it, drink Rain-water, which gives rise to the merry saying, that a Dutchman's Mouth is for ever open, either to swallow down Smoke or to drink up Rain. And indeed they are a wide-gaping Generation.

Being as yet a Bachelor, I agreed for my Lodging and Victuals with Mr. Vandepeereboom, who had a fair House, very stately, on one of the Canals behind the Heeren Gragt, or Lord's Street. 'Twould have had quite a princely appearance, but for a row of Elms in front, which, with their fan, almost concealed the Mansion. The noble look of the House, too, was somewhat spoilt by its being next door to a shop where they sold Drugs; which like all others of this trade in Holland, had for a sign a huge Carved Head, with the mouth wide open, in front of the window: sometimes it rudely resembles a Mercury's Head, and at other times has a Fool's Cap upon it.

This clumsy sign is called *de Gaaper*,—the Gaper,—and I know not the origin of it. Some of the Shop-boards they call *Uithang Borden*, and have ridiculous Verses written upon them; and 'tis singular to mark how much of the Jackpudding these Dutchmen, who are keener than Jews in their Cash-matters, have in them.

Mr. Vandepeereboom was high in the College of Magistrates, and I was ofttimes privileged to witness with him the adminis-tration of Justice and the infliction of its Dread Awards,—all here very Decent and Solemn. The Awful Sentence of Death is delivered in a room on the basement-floor of the Stadt House: the entrance through a massy folding-door covered with brass Em-blems, such as Jove's Beams of Lightning, and Flaming Swords; above, between the Rails, are the old and new City Arms; and at the bottom are Death's Heads and Bones. The inside of the Hall, mighty handsome, in white Marble, and proper History pieces of the Judgment of Solomon, and Zeleucus the Locrian King tearing out one of his

Eyes to save one of his Son's, and Junius Brutus putting his children to Death. On the fore part of the Judgment-seat a fine Marble Statue of Silence, gallantly, but quite falsely, represented by the figure of a Woman on the ground, her finger to her lips, and two Children by her, Weeping over a Death's Head. When the dire Doom of Death is about to be pronounced, the Criminal is brought into this Hall, guarded; and nothing is omitted in point of solemnity to impress on his mind (poor wretch!) and on those about him the awful consequences of violating the Laws of the Country; which is a much better mode, I think, of striking Terror into 'em than the French way, where the Magistrates settle the Sentence among themselves in private, and the *Greffier* comes all of a sudden into the unhappy Person's Cell to tell him that he is to be presently Executed; or even our Old Bailey fashion (though the Black Cap is frightful), where the Culprit is more or less sent to Hang like a Dog,—one down, another come up; and Jack Ketch Drunk all the while with burnt Brandy. 'Twas a thorough knowledge of Human Nature, too, that thought of placing this Dutch hall of Justice on the ground-floor, and its Brazen Door opening into a common Thoroughfare through the Stadt House. I never passed by this door without seeing numbers of the Lower Orders of people gazing wistfully through the Rails upon the emblematic objects within, apparently in Melancholy Meditation, and reflecting upon the Ignominious Effects of deviating from the Paths of Virtue.

Out of the Burgomaster's parlour in the same building is a passage to the Execution Chamber, or Hall of the Last Prayers, where the Condemned take leave of their Clergy, and pass through a Window, the lower part of Wood, so that it opens level with the the floor of the Scaffold, which is constructed on the outside, opposite the Waag or Weigh House.

As associate of one of the Magistrates, I often visited the Dungeons beneath the Stadt House, which are hermetically Sealed unto all Strangers. As places of Confinement, nothing can be more secure; as places of punishment, nothing more Horrible. Here, by the faint light of a Rush Candle, you gaze only on Emaciated Figures, while out of the Dark Shadows issue faint but dismal Groans. Some are here condemned to linger for Life; yet have I known convicted Creatures in this Rat's hole as merry as French Dancing-Masters, whistling, trolling, and gambolling in the Dark; while in the next cell were a number of Women, who, like the general of their sex when in Durance, did nothing but Yell and tear their Clothes to Pieces. But 'tis true that all confined in these dreadful places had committed crimes of a very Malignant nature, and which heartily warranted their being thus cut off from Light and Air, and immured in Regions fit only to be Receptacles for the Dead. Under the Hall of Justice is likewise the Torture Chamber, where Miserable Creatures, at the bidding of their Barbarous Judges, undergo a variety of Torments; one of which is to fasten the Hands behind the Neck with a cord through pulleys secured to the vaulted Ceiling, so as to be jerked up and down. Weights of Fifty Pounds each are then suspended to the Feet, until anguish overpowers the senses, and a Confession of Guilt is heard to quiver on the lips. Public Punishments are inflicted only Four Times a Year, when a vast Scaffold is erected in the Space between the Stadt House and Waag House, as before mentioned. Those that are only to be Whipped endure that compliment with Merciless Severity, and are not permitted to Retire till those who are to Die have suffered, which is either by Decapitation or by the Rope. And this acts as a Warning as to what will happen to 'em next time. On this occasion the Chief Magistrates attend in their Robes. But though Strict, they are mighty Just in administering their Laws, and will not permit the least deviation or aggravation of the Sentence meted out. I did hear of one jocular Rogue, that was condemned, for the murder of half-a-dozen women and children, to have his Head severed from the Trunk at one stroke of the Sword. This Mynheer

Merry-Andrew, previous to quitting the Prayer Chamber, lays a Wager with a Friend that the Executioner should not be able to perform his office according to the exact terms of the Sentence. So, the moment he knelt to receive the Fatal Stroke, he rolled his Head in every direction so violently and rapidly, that the Headsman could not hit him with any chance of severing his Neck at once; and after many fruitless aims, was obliged to renounce the Task. The Officers who were to see the Sentence executed were now in a Great Dilemma. In vain did they try by argument to persuade the Fellow to remain still, and have his Head quietly taken off. At last he was remanded back to Prison, and after an hour's deliberation the presiding Magistrate, upon his own Responsibility, ordered the Gallows to be brought out, and the Fellow to be straightway Hanged thereupon; which was done, to the contentment of the Populace, who were howling with Rage at the fear of being deprived of their Sport. But the strait-laced Dutch Judges and Lawyers all took alarm, and declared that the Fellow had been murdered; and nothing but the high rank and character of the Magistrate preserved him from grievous consequences.

They observe, however, degrees in their Punishments, and are, even in extreme cases, averse from Bloodshed, and willing to try all ways with a criminal before Hanging or Beheading him. Thus have they their famous Rasphuys for the Confinement and Correction of those whose Crimes are not capital. Over the Gate are some insignificant painted wooden figures, representing Rogues sawing Log-wood, and Justice holding a Rod over them; and the like of these, with figures of scourging and branding, they stick up in their Public Walks and Gardens, to show what is Done to those who pluck the Flowers or carve Names upon the Trunks of the Trees, and it has a most wholesome effect in frightening Evil-doers. So in the Yard of the Rasphuys is a Whipping-post in Terrorem, with another little figure of Justice flagrant with Execution. Here the Rogues saw Campeachy-wood, which seems to be most toilsome work; and yet by practice they can saw Two Hundred Pounds' weight every week with ease, and also make many little Articles in Straw, Wood, Bone, and Copper, to sell to Visitors. They are all clad in White Woollen, which, when they are stained with the Red Sawdust, gives them a Hobgoblin kind of appearance. Here too, in a corner of the Yard, they show the Cell in which if the person who was confined in it did not incessantly Pump out the Water let into it, he must inevitably be Drowned; but this Engine, the Gaolers said, had not been used for many Years, and was only kept up as an object of Terror.

In the east quarter of Amsterdam, Justice is administered in its mildest form; there being the Workhouse close to the Muider Gragt, a place which, I believe, has not its parallel in the whole World. 'Tis partly Correctional and partly Charitable; and when I saw it, there were Seven Hundred and Fifty Persons within the Walls, the yearly expense being about One Hundred Thou-

sand Florins.   In the rooms belonging to
the Governors and Directresses some ex-
quisite Paintings by Van Dyck, Rembrandt,
and Jordaens; and, indeed, you can go
scarcely any where in Holland, from a Pig-
stye to a Palace, without finding Paintings.
Here, in a vast room very cleanly kept, are
an immense number of Women occupied in
Sewing and Spinning.   Among them I saw
once a fine hearty-looking Irishwoman, who
had been Confined here two whole Years,
for being a little more fond of true Schiedam
Gin than her lawful Spouse.   In another
vast Apartment, secured by many Iron Rail-
ings and Grated Windows, are the Female
Convicts in the highest state of Discipline,
and very industriously and silently engaged
in making Lace, under the superintendence
of a Governess.   From the Walls of the
Room are suspended Instruments of Punishment, such as Scourges, Gags, and Manacles,
the which are not spared upon the slightest
appearance of Insubordination.   Then there
are Wards for the Men, Schoolrooms for a
vast number of Children, and Dormitories,

all in the highest state of Neatness. In
another part of the Building, which only
the Magistrates are permitted to visit, are
usually detained ten or a dozen Young Ladies
—some of very high Families—sent here by
their Parents or Friends for undutiful De-
portment, or some other Domestic Offence.
They are compelled to wear a particular
Dress as a mark of Degradation ; are kept
apart ; forced to work a certain number of
hours a day ; and are occasionally Whipped.
Here, too, upon complaints of Extravagance,
Tipsiness, &c., duly proved, can Husbands
send their Wives, to be confined and receive
the Discipline of the House ; *and hither, too,
can Wives send their Husbands for the same
Cause, for Two, Three, and Four Years together, till they show signs of amended Behaviour.*
The Food is abundant, and good ; but the
Work is hard, and the Stripes are many.
Might not such a course be tried with
advantage in England, to abate and cure
the frivolities and extravagances of Fashion-
able People ?

So then, as an Honourable Merchant in a

city and country where Commerce is reckoned among the noblest of Pursuits, I might, but for my Perverse Fate, have grown Rich, and taken unto myself a Dutch Wife, and had a Brood of little Broad-beamed Children, that should smoke their Tobacco and quaff their Schiedam, even from their Cradle upwards. Indeed, Madam Vanderkipperhaerin of Gouda (the place where the Cows feed in the Meadows clad in Blue-striped Jackets and Petticoats) was pleased to look upon me with Eyes of Favour, and often said it was a Sin and Shame that such a Proper Man as I (as she was good enough to say) was not Married and Settled. And, indeed, why not? I ofttimes asked myself. I had Florins, Guilders, and Stuyvers in abundance ; my Partner was a Magistrate, and well reputed worthy : why should I not give Hostages to Fortune, and have done for good and all with the Life of a Roving Bachelor ? By this time (although by no means forgetting my own dear native Tongue) I spoke French with Ease and Fluency, if not with Grammatical correctness ; and had likewise an indifferently copious acquaintance with the Hollands Dialect. Why should not I be a Magistrate, a Burgomaster? Madam Vanderkipperhaerin was Rich, and had a beautiful Summer Villa all glistening with Bee's-waxed Campeachy-wood and Polished Brass on the River Amstel, some three miles from the City. She had a whole Cabinet full of Ostades and Jan Steens in ebony frames, and a Side-board of Antique Plate that might have made Cranbourn Alley jealous. Why did not I avail myself of the many Propitious Moments that offered, and demand the Hand of that most respectable Dutch Dame.

The Melancholy Truth is, that she chose to be jealous of Betje, Mr. Vandepeereboom's comely Housekeeper, upon whom I declare that I had never cast any thing but innocently Paternal Glances, and utterly deny that I ever foregathered with that young Fraw. She was for moving Mr. Vandepeereboom to have Betje sent to the Workhouse, there to be set to Spinning, and to receive the usual unhandsome Treatment; and when he refused,—having, in truth, no fault to find with the Poor Girl,—Madam, in a Huff, withdrew her Countenance and Favour from me, and, with sundry of her spiteful gossips, revived the old Story of my having several Wives alive in different parts of Europe and the New World. Surely there was never yet a man so exposed to calumny as poor John Dangerous !

Then, to make matters worse, there came that sad Affair of the Beguine. Flesh and blood ! a mortal man (I suppose) is not to be reckoned among the vilest of Humanity because he falls in Love. How could I help Wilhelmina van Praag being a Beguine? Moreover, a Beguine is not a Nun. The Beguines belong to a modified kind of Monastic Order. They reside in a large House with a wall and ditch around it, and that has a Church and Hospital inside, and is for all the world like a little Town. But the Sisterhood is perfectly secular ; they mingle with the inhabitants of the city, quit the Convent when they choose, and even marry when they are so minded ; but they are obliged, so long as they belong to the

Order, to attend Prayers a certain number of times a day, and to be within the Convent-walls at a stated hour every evening. To be admitted to this Order, they must be either unmarried or widows without children; and the only certificate required of them is that of Good Behaviour, and that they have a Competence to live upon. You may ask, if this almost entire Liberty be granted them, what there was to hinder Mynheer Jan van Dangerous and the Fair Beguine Wilhelmina van Praag from coming together as Man and Wife? Wilhelmina was the comeliest Creature (save one) that I have ever seen; and, but that she was a little Stout, would have passed as the living model for the St. Catherine which Signor Raphael the Painter did so well in Oils. I don't think I loved her; but she took my Fancy immensely, and meeting her in the houses of divers Honourable Families in Amsterdam, 'tis not to be concealed that I courted her with much assiduity. This, by some mischief-making Persons, was held to be highly compromising to the Fair Beguine.

For all that I had become a Grave Merchant, there was yet somewhat of the Gentleman of the Sword and Adventurer on the High Seas about me; and a great hulking Cousin of the young Fraw, that was a Lieutenant in their High Mightinesses Land Forces, —the Amphibious Grenadiers I call 'em, and more used to Salt-water than Salt-petre,—must needs challenge me to the Duello. The laws against private warfare being very strict in Holland, we were obliged to make a journey into Austrian Flanders, to Arrange our Difficulty; and meeting on the borders of the Duchy of Luxembourg, I— Well, is Jack Dangerous to be blamed for that he was, in the prime of Life, an approved Master of Fence?

The Lieutenant being dead of his Wounds (received in perfectly fair fight), the whole City of Amsterdam must needs cry out that I had murdered the Man; and the Families who had once been eager to receive me turned their backs upon me. Then the Fair Beguine must go into a craze; and, upon my word, when I heard how Mad she was, and how they had been obliged to shut her up in the Hospital, I could not help thinking of the History of my Grandmother, and did mistrust meeting the young Fraw van Praag again (for she was very Sweet, I believe, with the Spark that forced me to fight with him), for fear that she should Pistol me. But she did not; and Recovered, to marry a very Wealthy Shipmaster named Druyckx.

While this Ugly Business was the talk of all tongues (but Mr. Vandepeereboom clapped me on the Shoulder, and bade me take my Diversion while he minded Business, for that all would Blow Over soon), I took an Excursion ('twas in the third year of my Residence here) into North Holland, to visit the famous village of Brock. Here the streets are divided by little Rivulets, for all the world like Lilliputian Canals; the Houses and Summer-houses all of Wood, painted Green and White, very handsome, albeit whimsical in their shape, and scrupulously neat. The Inhabitants have a peculiar association among themselves, and scarcely

ever admit a Stranger within their Doors.
During my stay I only saw the Faces of two
of 'em, and then only by a stealthy Peep.
They are said to be very rich, and in some
of their Kitchens to have Pots and Pans of
solid Gold. The Shutters of the Windows
always kept closed, and the Householders go
to and fro by a Back Door, the Principal
Entrance being opened only at Marriages
and Deaths. The Street Pavement all set
out with Pebbles and Cockleshells, and no
Dogs or Cats were seen to trespass upon
it; and formerly there was a law to oblige
all Passengers to take off their Shoes.
Here it was that a Man was once Convened
and Reprimanded for Sneezing in the
Streets; and, latterly, a Parson, I heard,
upon being appointed to fill the Church on
the Demise of an old Predecessor, gave great
offence to his Flock for not taking off his
Shoes when he ascended the Pulpit. The
Gardens of this strange Village produce Deer,
Dogs, Peacocks, Chairs, and Ladders, all cut
out in Box. I never saw such a Museum of
vegetable Statuary in my Life before. On

the whole, Brock resembles a trim, sprightly Ball-room, all garnished, lighted up, and the floor well chalked, but not a Soul to Scrape Fiddle or Foot Minuet. Farther from here is Saardam, which, at a distance, looks like a City of Windmills.

Item.——I forgot to say, that at Brock they tie up the Cows' Tails with Blue Ribbons.

The Houses of Saardam are principally built of Wood, and every one has a Fantastic kind of Baby Garden. Here is the Wooden Hut where Peter the Great lived, when he wrought as a Shipwright in the Navy-yard. It stands in a Garden, and is in Decent Preservation. The women in North Holland are said to be handsomer than in any other part of the country ; but I was out of taste with Beauty when I came hither, and could see naught but ugly Faces.

So, coming back to Amsterdam, I found that Mr. Vandepeereboom's Prediction was fulfilled with a Vengeance, and with Compound Interest. The Business of the Beguine had

Blown Over; but another affair had Blown On, and this very speedily ended in a Blow Up. I am sorry to say that this Fairspoken and seemingly Reputable Mr. Vandepeereboom turned out to be a very Great Rogue. Our Firm was in the Batavian trade, dealing in fine Spices, Nutmegs, Cloves, Mace, Cinnamon, and so forth; also in Rice, Cotton, and Pepper; and especially in the Java Coffee, which is held to be second only to that of Arabia. In this branch of Trade the Dutch have no competition, and they are able to keep the price of their Spices as high as they choose, by ordering what remains unsold at the price they have fixed upon it to be Burnt. How it came to pass that the Spice Ships consigned to us were all wrecked on the High Seas and never insured; that the Batavian Merchants, to whom we advanced money on their Consignments, all failed dismally; that every Speculation we entered into went against us, and that we always burnt our Surplus Goods just as prices were about to rise,—I know not; but certain it is, that I had not been

three weeks back in Amsterdam before the
House of Vandepeereboom and Dangerous
went Bankrupt.   Now 'tis an ugly thing to
be Bankrupt in Holland.   The people are
so thrifty and persevering, and so jealous of
keeping their Engagements, that the very
rarity of Insolvency makes it Scandalous.
A Trading Debtor being a character very
seldom to be met with, he is held in more
Odium in Holland than in any other part of
Europe.   Yet are their Laws of Arrest
milder than with us in England, where for
a matter of Forty Shillings an Honest Man
becomes the prey of a Catchpole, and for
years after he has paid the Debt itself, with
exorbitant Costs to some Knavish Limb of
the Law, may still continue to Rot in Gaol
for the Keeper's Fees or Garnish.   Here,
if the Debtor be a Citizen or Registered
Burgher (as I was), he is not subject to
have his Person seized at the suit of his
Creditors, until three regular Summonses
have been duly served upon him to appear
in the Court, which Processes are completed
in about a month; after which, if he does

not obey it, he may be laid hold of, but only when he has quitted his House; for in Holland a Man's Dwelling is held even more sacred than in England, and no Writ or Execution whatever is capable of being served upon him so long as he keeps close, or even if he stands on the threshold of his Home. . In this Sanctuary he may set at Defiance every Claimant; but if he have the Hardihood to appear Abroad, the Sergeants collar him forthwith. But even in this case he goes not to a common Gaol or Prison for Felons, but to a House of Restriction, where he is properly entreated, and maintained with Liberal Humanity; the Expense of which, as well as the Proceedings, must all be defrayed by the Creditors. This regards only the private Gentleman Debtor; but woe betide the Fraudulent Trader! The Bankrupt Laws of Holland differ from ours in this respect, that all the Creditors must sign the Debtor's Certificate, or Agreement of Liberation. If any decline, the Ground of their Refusal is submitted to Arbitrators, who decide as to the merits of the case; and

if the Broken Merchant be found to be a
Cheat, no Mercy is shown him.   The Rasphuys, the Pillory, nay, even the Dungeons
beneath the Stadt House, may be his
Doom.

This, Mr. Vandepeereboom (being a born
Dutchman) knew very well ; and he waited
neither for Deliberations as to his Certificate,
nor for Arbitrators' award.   He e'en showed
his Creditors a clean Pair of Heels, and took
Shipping for Harwich in England.   I
believe he afterwards prospered exceedingly
in London as a Crimp, or Purveyor of Men
for the Sea-Service, and submitted to the
East India Company many notable plans
for injuring the Commerce of the Hollanders.
I have likewise reason to think that he did
me a great deal of harm amongst my late
Owners at Bristol and elsewhere, saying that
I had been the Ruin of him with Wasteful
Extravagance and Deboshed Ways, and that
but for his Intercession I should have been
Broken on the Wheel for unhandsome
Behaviour to the Fair Beguine.   Ere he
flitted, he left me a Letter, in which he had

the Impudence to tell me that he had long since drawn out my Account from the Bank of Amsterdam, thinking himself much better able to take care of the Money than I was. Furthermore he contemptuously advised me to try some other line than Commerce, for which I was, through my Former Career— or Vagabond Habits, as he had the face to call it—in no wise Fitted. Finally, he ironically wished me a Good Deliverance from the hands of the Assessors of the Commercial Tribunal, and, with a Devilish Sneer, recommended his Housekeeper Betje to my care. O Mr. Vandepeereboom, Mr. Vandepeereboom! if ever we meet again, old as I am, there shall be Weeping in Holland for you—if, indeed, there be anybody left to shed tears for such a Worthless Rascal.

This most Dishonest Person, however, did me unwittingly a trifle of good, and at all events saved me from Gyves and Stripes. That Passage of his in the Letter about my Funds in the Bank of Amsterdam was my Deliverance. 'Twas widely known that I was but a simple Seafaring Man, unused to

Mercantile Affairs, and that I had really brought with me the considerable Sum of Twenty Hundred Pounds. I was arrested, it is true, and lay for many Months in the House of Restriction; but interest was made for me, and the Creditors of the Broken House agreed to sign a Certificate of Liberation. I believe that but for that mournful business of the Beguine, and for that confounded Officer that I sworded, some of the Wealthy Merchants would have subscribed to an Association for setting me up again; but that Rencounter was remembered to my hurt, and, says Mynheer van Bommel, when he brought me my Certificate, " Hark ye, Friend Englander; you are Free this time. Take my advice, and get you out of Holland as quick as ever you can; for their High Mightinesses, to say nothing of the Worshipful Burgomasters of this City, have a misliking for Men that are too quick with the Sword and too slow with the Pen; and if you don't speedily mend your way of Life, and bid farewell to this Country, you will find yourself sawing of

Campeachy-wood at the Rasphuys, with Dirk Juill, the Beadle, standing over you with a Thong." Upon which I thanked him heartily; and he had the Generosity to lend me Fifty Florins to furnish my present needs.

I was no longer a Young Man. I was now long past my fortieth year, again almost a Pauper, Friendless and Unknown in the World; yet did I feel Undaunted, and confident that Better Days were in store for me. Pouching my Fifty Florins, I first followed the Burgomaster's advice by getting out of Holland as quick as ever I could, and betook myself by Treyckshuyt and Stage Wagon to the city of Bruxelles in Brabant. Here I abode for some months in the house of a clean Widow-woman that was a Walloon, who, finding that I was English, and, besides, a very tolerable French Scholar, procured me several Pupils among the Tradesfolk in the neighbourhood of the Petit Sablon (hard by the Archduchess Governante's Palace), where I dwelt on a Sixth Floor. By degrees I did so increase my number of

Pupils, that I was able to open a School of
some thirty Lads and Lasses. To both
indifferently I taught the Languages, with
Writing and Accompts; while for the instruction of the latter in Needlework and
other Feminine Accomplishments I engaged
my Landlady's Daughter, a comely Maiden,
albeit Red-haired, and very much pitted with
the Small-pox. Figure to yourself Captain
Jack Dangerous turned Dominie! I am
venturesome enough to believe that I was a
very passable Pedagogue; and of this I am
certain, that I was entirely beloved by my
Scholars. The sufferings I had undergone
while a Captive in the hands of that Barbarous Wretch, Gnawbit, had never been
effaced from my Memory, and had made me
infinitely tender towards little Children.
Indeed I could scarcely bear to use the
Ferula to them, or nip 'em with a Fescue,
much less to untruss and Scourge 'em, as 'tis
the brutal fashion of Pedants to do; nor do
I think, though I disobeyed Solomon's
maxim, and Spared the Rod, that I did much
towards Spoiling any Child that was under

my care. I made Learning easy and pleasant to my Youngsters, by telling them all sorts of moving and marvellous Stories, drawn from what Books of History I had handy (and these I admit I coloured a little, to suit the Imaginations of the Young), and others concerning my own remarkable Adventures, in which, however extraordinary they seemed, I always took care to adhere strictly to the Truth, only suppressing that which it was not proper for Youth and Innocence to be made acquainted with.

But Schoolkeeping is a tiresome trade. One cannot be at it day and night too ; and a Man must have some place to Divert himself in, when the toils of the day are over. I found out a Coffee-House in the Rue de Merinos, or Spaan Scheep Straet, as the Flemings call it, in strange likeness to our tongue, and there, over my Tobacco, made some strange Acquaintance. There was one De Suaso, an Empiric, that had writ against the English College of Physicians, and was like to have made a Fortune by his famous Nostrum for the Gout, *the Sudorific Expulsive*

Mixture; but that Scheme had fallen through, it having been discovered that the Mixture was naught but Quicksilver and Suet, which made the Patients perspire indeed, but turned 'em all, to the very Silver in their Pockets, as Black as Small-Coal Men. Now, he had become a kind of Pedlar, selling Handkerchiefs made at Amsterdam, in imitation of those of Naples, with Women's Gloves, Fans, Essences, and Pomatums—and in fact all the Whim-Whams that are known in the Italian trade as *Galanterie le più curiose di Venezia e di Milano.* But his prime trade was in Selling of Snuff, for the choicer sorts of which there was at that time a perfect Rage among the Quality, both of the Continent and of England. This De Suaso used to Laugh, and say that the best venture he had ever made was from a Parcel of Snuff so bad and rotten, that he was about to send it back to the Hamburg Merchant who had sold it him, when one day, plying at the chief Coffee-House, as was his wont, my Lord Hautgoustham, an English Nobleman, desired him to fill his box with the choicest Snuff he had. Thinking my Lord really a Judge, he gives him some undeniable *Bouquet Dauphine ;* but the Peer would have none of it. Then he tries him with one Mixture after another, but always unsuccessfully ; until at last he bethinks him of the Musty Parcel he has at home, and accordingly, having fetched some of that, returns to the Coffee-House, and says that he has indeed a Snuff of extraordinary Smell and Taste, but that 'tis extravagantly dear. Lord Hautgoustham tries it, and calls out in an ecstasy that 'tis the most beautiful Snuff he ever put to his Nose. He bought a Pound of it, for which De Suaso charged him at the moderate rate of Four Guineas ; and desires to know his Lodging, that he may send his Friends to buy some of this Incomparable Mixture. The Artful Rogue then affects the Coy, says that his Stock of the Snuff is very low, and by degrees raises his price to Eleven Pistoles a Pound, until the English in Brussels have been half-poisoned with his filthy Remnant ; when there comes upon the scene a certain

Mr. Dubiggin, a rich old English Merchant of the Caraccas, who knew all kinds of Snuff as well as a Yorkshire Tyke knows Horses; and he, telling the Nobleman and his Friends how they have been duped, my Lord Haut-goustham, who was of a hot temper, makes no more ado, but kicks this unhappy De Suaso half way down the Montagne de la Cour.

Here, too, I made an Acquaintance who was afterwards the means of working me much Mischief. This was one Ferdinando Carolyi, that said he was a Styrian, but spoke most Tongues, and was a thoroughly accomplished Rascal. He had been a painter of Flower-pieces, and from what I could learn had also made the Mill to go in the way of coining False Money; but at the time I knew him was all for the occult Science called the Cabala. He showed me a whole chestful of Writings at his Lodgings—which were very mean—and declared that he had invented a perfect and particular System, which he called the Astronomical Terrestrial Cabala. He had run through the whole Pentateuch, and had reduced to the Signs of the Zodiac the words of such Scripture Verses as answered to the same ; one to Aries, the second to Taurus, the third to Gemini, and the like. In short, there appeared a kind of Harmony in 'em, particularly when the Terrestrial Cabala (which was of the Dryest) was moistened with a flask or two of good old Rhenish. The whole of this contrivance was to tend towards the Discovery of the Philosopher's Stone. He pretended by these Astronomical Figures to have penetrated into the most essential Arcana of Nature, and all the necessary operations for attaining the *Elixir Philosophorum*, or some such word. But this Carolyi had such a winning Way with him, that he would well-nigh have talked a Donkey's Hind-leg off. He began to tell me about Peter of Lombardy and the great adept Zacharias, -and of the blessed Terra Foliata, or Land of Leaves, where Gold is sown to be radically Dissolved in order to its Putrefaction and Regermination in a Fixation which has Power over its Brethren the Imperfect Metals, and makes them like unto itself; and this process (which I believe to have been only a story about a Cock and a Bull) he called Re-incrudation.   In fact my Gentleman almost talked me out of my Senses : and as I thought him a monstrous clever Man, I lent him (although my Purse was as lean as might be) half-a-score of Austrian Ducats, to carry out his experiments in the Universal Menstruum.   Alas ! I never saw my Ducats nor my Alchemist again.   A week after I had lent him the money, he fled on a suspicion of Base Coin ; and I had hard work to persuade the Officers of Justice that I had not a hand in his Malpractices.   As it was, nearly all my Scholars fell away from my School; and the Impudent Flemings sneered at me as *Mozzoo Kabala,*—in their barbarous Lingo,—and I was pointed out in the streets as a Wizard, a Fortune-teller, a Cunning Man, and what not.   So that I was fain, after about ten years' sojourn at Bruxelles, to call in my Dues, gather my few Effects together, and bidding farewell to Flanders, proceed to Paris. It was time ; for the Priests were up in arms against me as a Heretic Outlaw, dealing in Magic. The Black Gentry are hereabouts very Bigoted; and although they have no Inquisition, would, I doubt not, have led me a sorry Life, but for my Discretion in timely Flitting.

CHAPTER THE FIFTH.

OF A STRANGE AND HORRIBLE ADVENTURE I HAD IN PARIS, WHICH WAS NEARLY MY UNDOING.

THE Manner of its Coming About was this. I arrived in Paris very Poor and Miserable, and was for some days (when that which I brought with me was spent) almost destitute of Bread.   At last, hearing that some Odd Hands were wanted at the Opera-House to caper about in a new Ballet upon the Story of Orpheus, the Master of the Tavern where I Lodged, who had been a Property-Master at the Theatres, and entertained many of the Playing Gentry, made interest for me, as much to keep me from Starving as to put me in the way of earning enough money to pay my Score to him.   For I have found that there never was in this world a man so Poor but he could manage to run into Debt. In virtue of his Influence, I, who had never so much as stood up in a polite Minuet in my life, and knew no more of Dancing than sufficed to foot it on a Shuffleboard at a Tavern to the tune of Green Sleeves, was engaged at the wages of one Livre ten Sols a night to be a Mime in the same Ballet. But 'twas little proficiency in Dancing they wanted from me. One need not have been bound 'prentice to a Hackney Caper-Merchant to play one of the Furies that hold back Eurydice, and vomit Flames through a Great Mask. They gave me a Monstrous Dress, akin to the *San Benitos* which are worn by the poor wretches who are burnt by the Inquisition; and my flame-burning was done by an Ingenious Mechanical Contrivance, that had a most delectable effect, albeit the Fumes of the Sulphur half-choked me. And they did not ask for any Characters for their Furies. I tumbled and vomited Flames for at least thirty nights, when one evening, standing at the Side-Scenes waiting for my turn to come on, it chanced that the light gauzy Coats of a pretty little Dancing-girl, that was playing a Dryad in the Wood where Orpheus charms the Beast, caught Fire. I think 'twas the Candle fell out of the Moon-box, and so on to her Drapery; but, at all events, she was Alight, and ran about the Scene, screaming piteously. The poor little cowardly wretches her Companions all ran away in sheer terror; and as for the two Musqueteers of the Guard who stood sentry at each side of the Proscenium, one dastard Losel fell on his Marrow-bones and began bawling for his Saints, whilst the other, a more active Craven, drops his musket and bayonet with a clang, and clambers into the Orchestra, hitting out right and left among the Fiddlers, and very nearly tumbling into the Big Drum. All this took much less time to pass than I have taken to relate; but as quick as thought I rushed on to the stage, seized hold of the little Dancing-girl, tripped her up, and rolling her over and over on the Boards, I encompassed her till the flames were Extinguished. Luckily there was no Harm done. She was Bruised all over, and one of her pretty little Elbows was scratched; but that was all. One of the Gentlemen of the King's Chamber came round from his Box; and the Sardinian Ambassador sends round at once a Purse of Fifty Pistoles, and an offer for her to become his Madam; "For I should like one," his Excellency said, "that had been half-roasted. All these Frenchwomen look as though they had been boiled." When the Little Girl was brought to her Dressing-room, and had somewhat recovered from her Fright, she began to thank me, her Preserver, as she called me, with great Fervour and Vehemence; yet did I fancy that, although her words were excellently well chosen, she spoke with somewhat of an English Accent. And indeed she proved to be English. She was the Daughter of one Mr. Lovell, an English Gentleman of very fair extraction, who had been unfortunately mixed up in the troubles of the Forty-five; and having been rather a dangerous Plotter, and so excepted from the Act of Oblivion, had been fain to reside in Paris ever since, picking up a Crust as he could by translating, teaching of the Theorbo and Harpsichord, and such-like sorry Shifts. But he was very well connected, and had powerful friends among the French Quality. He was now a very old man, but of a most Genteel Presence and Majestic Carriage. The Little Girl's name—she was now about Eighteen years old—was Lilias, and she was the only one. As she had a marvellous turn for Dancing, old Mr. Lovell had (in the stress of his Affairs) allowed her to be hired at the Opera House, where she received no less than a Hundred Ecus a month; but he knew too well what mettle Gentlemen of the King's Chamber and Musqueteers of the Guard were made of; and every night after the Performance he came down to the Theatre to fetch her—his Hat fiercely cocked, and his long Sword under his arm. So that none dared follow or molest her. And I question even, if he had heard of the Ambassador's offer, whether the old Gentleman would not have demanded Satisfaction from his Excellency for that slight.

When I discovered that this dear little Creature, who was as fair as her name and as good as gold, was my Countrywoman, I made bold to tell her that I was English too; whereupon she Laughed, and in her sweet manner expressed her wonder that I had come to be playing a Fury at the French Opera House. I chose to keep my Belongings private for the nonce; so the old Gentleman, treating me as an honest fellow of Low Degree, presented me with ten Livres, which I accepted, nothing loth, and the Theatre People even made a purse for me amounting to Fifty more. So that I got as rich as a Jew, and was much in favour with my Landlord. But, better than all, the Little Girl, as I was her Preserver, insisted that I should be her Protector too; and old Mr. Lovell being laid up very bad with the rheumatism, I was often privileged to attend her home after the Theatre, walking respectfully a couple of paces behind her, and grasping a stout Cudgel. Father and Daughter lived in the Impasse Mauvaise Langue, Rue des Moineaux, behind St. Rogue's Church; and often when I had got my precious charge home, she would press me to stop to supper, the which I took very humbly at a side table, and listened to the stories of old Mr. Lovell (who was very garrulous) about the Forty-five. "Bless his old heart," thought I; "I could tell him something about the Forty-five that would astonish him."

'Twas one night after leaving the Impasse Mauvaise Langue that, feeling both cold and dry, I turned into a Tavern that was open late, for a measure of Hot Spiced Wine, as a Night-cap. There was no one there, beyond the People of the House, save a man in a Drugget coat, a green velveteen Waistcoat, red plush Nethers, and a flapped Hat, all very Worn and Greasy. He was about my own age, and wore his own Hair; but the most remarkable thing about him was his Face. I never saw such a Red Face. 'Twas a hundred times more fiery than that of Bardolph in the Play. 'Twas more glowing than a Salamander's. 'Twas redder than Sir Robert Walpole's (the great Whig Minister who, in my youth, was called by the Common "Brandy-faced Bob!"). This man's Face was most terribly puffed and swollen, and the veins all injected with purplish Blood. The tips of his Ears were like two pendant Carbuncles. His little bloodshot Eyes seemed starting from their Sockets, while the Cheeks beneath puffed out like Pillows for his Orbits to rest upon. Not less worthy of remark was it that this Red-faced Man's Lips were of a tawny White. He was for ever scrabbling with his hands among his tufted Locks, and pressing them to his Temples, as though his Head pained him—which there was reason to believe it did.

This strange Person was, when I entered the Wine-shop, in hot Dispute with the Master about some trifling Liquor Score. He would not Pay, he said; no, not he. He had been basely Robbed and Swindled. He had plenty of Money, but he would not

disburse a Red Liard.   He showed, indeed,
a Leathern Purse with two or three Gold
Pieces in it, and smaller Money; but declared that he would Die sooner than disburse.   And as he said this, he drew out of
his pocket a long Clasp-Knife, two-bladed;
and opening it, brandished it about, and
said they had better let him go, or Worse
would come of it.

The Master of the Tavern and his Wife,
decent bodies both, were wofully frightened
at the behaviour of this Desperado; but I
was not to be frightened by such Racketing.
I bade him put up his Toothpick, giving
him at the same time a Back-Hander, which
drove him into a Corner, where he crouched,
snarling like a Wild-beast, but offering to
do me no hurt.   Then I asked what the
To-do was about, and was told that he stood
indebted but for Eight Sols, for Half a Litre
of Wine, and that they could not account
for his Fury.   The Man was evidently not
in Liquor, which was strange.

These good people were so flustered at
the Man's uncommon Demeanour, that, see-

ing I was Strong and Valiant, they begged me to take him away. This I did, first discharging his Reckoning; for as he had Money about him, I doubted not but that he would recoup me. I got him into the Street (which was close to the Market of the Innocents, and I lived in the Street of the Ancient Comedy, t'other side of the River), and asked him where he was going.

"To get a Billet of Confession," he made answer.

"Stuff and Nonsense!" I answered, in the French Tongue. "They sell them not at this Hour of Night. Where do you live?"

"In the Parvis of Notre Dame," says he, staring like a Stuck Pig. "O Arnault! O Jansenius! O Monsieur de Paris! all this is your fault!"

And he lugs out of his Pocket a ragged Sheet of Paper, which he said was the last Mandement or Charge of the Archbishop of Paris, and was for reading it to me by the Moonlight; but I stopped him short. I had heard in a vague manner that the

M 2

Public Mind was just then much agitated
by some Dispute between the Clergy and
the Parliament concerning Billets or Certifi-
cates of Confession; but they concerned
neither me nor the Opera House.   Besides,
an Hour after Midnight is not the time for
reading Archbishops' Charges in the Public
Streets.

"'Tis my belief, Brother," I said, as
soothingly as I could, "that you'd better
go Home, and tie a Wet Clout round your
Head; or, better still, hie to a Chirurgeon
and be let Blood.   Have you e'er a
Home?"

He began to tell me that his Name was
ROBERT FRANÇOIS DAMIENS; that he had
come from Picardy; that he had been a
Stableman, a Locksmith, a Camp-follower,
and a Servant at the College of Louis-le-
Grand; that he had a Wife who was a Cook
in a Noble Family, and a Daughter who
coloured Prints for a Seller of Engravings.
In short, he told me all save what I desired
to know.   And in the midst of his rambling

recital he stops, and claps his Hand to his Forehead again.

" What ails you ?" I asked.

" *C'est le Sang, c'est le Sang qui me monte à la Tête !*" cries he. " *La Faute est à Monseigneur et à son Mandement. Je périrai ; mais les Grands de la Terre périront avec moi.*"*

And with this Bedlamite Speech he broke away from me,—for I had kept a slight hold of him,—and set off Running as hard as his legs could carry him.

I concluded that this Red-faced Man must be some Mad Fellow just escaped out of Charenton ; and, having other Fish to fry, let him follow his own devices. Whereupon I kindled a Pipe of Tobacco, and went home to Bed.

---

* " 'Tis the Blood, the Blood mounting to my Head! 'Tis the Archbishop's fault, and that of his Charge. I shall perish ; but the Mighty Ones of the Earth shall perish with me."

I have, contrary to my practice, given these Words as they were spoken, in the French Tongue : for they sunk into my Mind, so as never to be forgotten.—J. D.

Two days after this (March, 1757), the whole Troop of the Opera House were commanded to Versailles, there to perform the Ballet of Orpheus before Mesdames the King's Daughters. I had by this time received slight Promotion, and played the Dog Cerberus,—at which my dear little Angel of a Lilias made much mirth. His Majesty was to have waited at Versailles for the playing of the Piece; but after Dinner he changes his mind, and determines on returning to his other Palace of Trianon.

'Twas about Five o'clock in the Afternoon, and there was a great Crowd in the Court of Marble to see the Most Christian King take Coach for Trianon. The Great Court was full of Gardes Françaises, Musqueteers Red and Gray carrying Torches, with Coaches, Led Horses, Prickers, Grooms, Pages, Valets, Waiting Women, and all the Hurley-Burly of a great Court. Some few of the Commonalty also managed to squeeze themselves in—amongst others, your humble

Servant, John Dangerous, who was now reckoned no better than a Rascal Buffoon.

'Twas bitterly cold, and freezing hard, and the Courtiers had their hands squeezed into great fur Muffs. I saw the King come down the Marble Staircase; a fair portly Gentleman, with a Greatcoat, lined with fur, over his ordinary vestments——then a novelty among the French, and called a *Redingote*, from our English Riding-coat.

"Is that the King?" I heard a Voice, which I seemed to remember, ask behind me, as the Monarch passed between a double line of Spectators to his Coach.

"Yes, Dog," answered he who had been addressed, and who was an Officer in the Gray Musqueteers. "Pig, why dost thou not take off thy Hat?"

I was all at once pushed violently on one side. A Man with a Drugget Coat and Flapped Hat, and whom I at once recognised by the light of the glaring torches as the Red-faced Brawler of the Wine-shop, darted through the line of Guards, an open

Knife in his hand, and rushing up to him, stabbed King Lewis the Fifteenth in the side.

I could hear his Majesty cry out, " *Oh! je suis blessé!*"——" I am wounded !"——but all the rest was turbulence and confusion; in the midst of which, not caring that the Red-faced Man should claim me as an Acquaintance, I slipped away. I need scarcely say that there was no Ballet at Versailles that night.

A great deal of Blood came from the King's Wound; for he was a Plethoric Sovereign, much given to High Living; but he was, on the whole, more Frightened than Hurt. Although when the Assassin was first laid hold of, His Majesty cried out in an Easy Manner that no Harm was to be done him, he never afterwards troubled his Royal Self in the slightest Manner to put a stop to the Hellish Torments inflicted on a Poor Wretch, who had, at the most, but scratched his Flesh, and for whom the most fitting Punishment would have been a Cell in a Madhouse.

As for this most miserable Red-faced Man, Robert François Damiens, this is what was done to him. At first handling, he was very nearly murdered by the Young Gentlemen Officers of the Body Guard, who, having tied him to a Bench, pricked him with their Sword Points, beat him with their Belts, and pummelled him about the Mouth with the Butt-ends of Pistols. Then he was had to the Civil Prison; and a certain President, named Michault, came to interrogate him, who being most zealous to discover whether the Parricide (as he was called) had any Accomplices, heated a Pair of Pincers in the Fire, and when they were red-hot, clawed and dragged away at the Unhappy Man's Legs, till the whole Dungeon did reek with the horrible Odour of Burnt Flesh. Just imagine one of our English Judges of the Land undertaking such a Hangman's Office! The poor Wretch made no other complaint than to murmur that the King had directed that he was not to be ill-treated; and when they further questioned him, could only stammer out some

Incoherent Balderdash about the Archbishop, the Parliament, and the Billets of Confession.

After many Days, he was removed from Versailles to Paris; but his Legs were so bad with the Burning, that they were obliged to carry him away on a Mattress. So to Paris; the Journey taking Six Hours, through his great attendance of Guards and the thickness of the Crowd. He was had to the Prison of the Conciergerie, and put into a Circular Dungeon in the Tower called of Montgomery—the very same one where Ravaillac, that killed Henry the Fourth, had formerly lain. There they put him into a kind of Sack of Shamoy Leather, leaving only his Head free; and he was tied down to his bed—which was a common Hospital Pallet—by an immense number of Leathern Straps, secured by Iron Rings to the Floor of his Dungeon. But what Dr. Goldsmith, the Poetry-writer, means by "Damiens' Bed of Steel," I'm sure I don't know. At the head and foot of his Bed an Exempt kept watch Night and Day, and every three-quarters of an hour the Guard was relieved; so that the Miserable Creature had little chance of Sleeping. He would have sunk under all this Cruelty, but that they kept him up with Rich Meats and Generous Wines, which they had all but to force down his Throat.

But while all this was being done to Damiens, other steps were being taken by Justice, the which narrowly concerned me. As he would denounce no Accomplices, real or imaginary, the Police did their best to find out his Confederates for themselves, and by diligent Inquiry made themselves acquainted with all Damiens' movements for days before he committed his Crime. They found out the Wine-shop where he had refused to pay his Reckoning and made a Disturbance; and learning from the people of the House what manner of Man had paid for him and taken him away, they were soon on *my* track. One night, just before the Ballet began, I was taken by two Exempts; and, in the very play-acting dress as Cerberus that I wore, was forced into a Sedan, and taken, surrounded by Guards, to the Prison of the Châtelet.   I thought of appealing to our Ambassador in Paris, and proving that I was a faithful Subject of King George; but, as it happened, I owed my safety to one who disowned that Monarch, and kept all his Allegiance for King James.   For old Mr. Lovell, hearing of my Arrest, and importuned by poor Pretty Miss Lilias, who was kind enough to shed many Tears on the occasion, hurried off to his Eminence the Cardinal de ——, who was all but supreme at Court, and with whom he had great Influence.   The Cardinal listens to him very graciously, and by and by comes down the President Pasquier to interrogate me, to whom I told a plain Tale, setting forth how I had been unfortunate in Business in Holland and Flanders, and was earning an honest Livelihood by playing a Dog in a Pantomime.   The people in the Wine-shop could not but bear me out in stating that I had come across the Red-faced Man by pure Accident, and was no Friend of his. It was moreover established by the Police, that I had not been seen in Damiens' company after the Night I first met him, and that I had a legitimate call to be at Versailles on the day of the Assassination; so that after about a fortnight's detention I was set at Liberty, to my own great joy and that of my good and kind Mistress Lilias, who had now repaid tenthousand-fold whatever paltry Service I had been fortunate enough to render her. Nay, this seeming Misadventure was of present service to me; for his Eminence was pleased to say that he should be glad to hear something more concerning me, for that I seemed a Bold Fellow; and at an Interview with him, which lasted more than an Hour, I told him my whole Life and Adventures, which caused him to elevate his Eyebrows not a little.

" *Cospetto!* Signor Dangerous," says he (for though he spoke French like a Native he was by Birth an Italian, and sometimes swore in that Language), " if all be true

what you say,—and you do not look like a
Man who tells Lies,—you have led a strange
Life. When a Boy, you were nearly
Hanged ; and now at the *mezzo cammin* of
Life you have been on the point of having
your Limbs broken on a St. Andrew's
Cross. However, we must see what we
can do for you. Strength, Valour, Expe-
rience, and Discretion do not often go
together ; but I give you credit for pos-
sessing a fair show of all Four. I suppose,
now, that you are tired of squatting at the
Wicket of the Infernal Regions at the
Opera House ?"

I bowed in acknowledgment of his
Eminence's compliments, and said that I
should be glad of any Employment.

"Well, well," continued his Eminence,
"we will see. At present, as you say you
are a fair Scholar, my Secretary will find
you some work in copying Letters. And
here, Signor Dangerous, take these ten
Louis, and furnish yourself with some more
Clerkly Attire than your present trim. It
would never do for a Prince of the Church

to have a Flavour of the Opera Side-Scenes about his house."

Unless Rumour lied, there hung sometimes about his Eminence's sumptuous hotel a Flavour, not alone of the Opera Side-Scenes, but of the Ballet-Dancers' Tiring-room. However, let that pass. I took the ten Louis with many Thanks, and six hours afterwards was strutting about in a suit of Black, full trimmed, with a little short Cloak, for all the world like a Notary's Clerk.

I had been in the Employ of his Eminence—who showed me daily more and more favour—about a month, when all Paris was agog with the News that the Monster Parricide and Hell-Hound (as they called him from the Pulpit), Robert François Damiens, was to suffer the last Penalty of his Crime. I know not what strange horrible fascination I yielded to, but I could not resist the desire to see the End of the Red-faced Man. I went. The Tragedy took place on the Place de Grêve; but ere he came on to his last Scene,

Damiens had gone through other Woes well-nigh unutterable. I speak not of his performing the *amende honorable*, bare-footed, in his Shirt, a Halter round his Neck, and a lighted Taper of six pounds' weight in his Hand, at the Church-door, confessing his Crime, and asking Pardon of God, the King, and all Christian Men. Ah! no; he had suffered more than this. Part of his Sentence was that, prior to Execution, he was to undergo the Question Ordinary and Extraordinary; and so at the Conciergerie, in the presence of Presidents, Counsellors of the Parliament, Great Noblemen of the Court, and other Dignitaries, the Poor Thing was put into the *Brodequins*, or Boots, and wedge after wedge driven in between his Legs—already raw and inflamed with the Devilries of the President Michault —and the Iron Incasement. He rent the air with his Screams, until the Surgeons declared that he could hold out no longer. But he confessed nothing; for what had he to confess?

Then came the last awful Day, when all

this Agony was to end. I saw it all. The Grêve was densely packed; and although the space is not a third so large as Tower Hill, there seemed to be Thousands more persons present than at the beheading of my Lord Lovat. A sorrier Sight was it to see the windows of the Hôtel de Ville thronged with Great Ladies of the Court, many of them Young and Beautiful, and all bravely Dressed, who laughed and chattered and ate Sweetmeats while the Terrible Show was going on. The Sentence ran that the Assassin's Hand, holding the Knife which he had used, should be Burnt in a Slow-fire of Sulphur. Then that his Flesh should be torn on the Breast, Arms, Stomach, Thighs, and Calves of the Legs with Pincers; and then that into the gaping Wounds there should be poured Melted Lead, Rosin, Pitch, Wax, and Boiling Oil. And finally, that by the Four Extremities he should be attached to Four Horses, and rent Asunder; his Body then to be Burnt, and his Ashes scattered to the Winds. There was nothing said about the Lord having mercy upon his

Soul ; but careful injunction was made that he was to be condemned in the Costs of the Prosecution.

All this was done, although I sicken to record it ; but in the most Blundering Butcherly manner. The Chief-Executioner of the Parliament was Sick, and so the task was deputed to his Nephew, Gabriel Sanson, who being, notwithstanding his Sanguinary Office (which is hereditary), a Humane kind of Young Man, was all in a Shiver at what he had to perform, and quite lost his Head. Both his Valets, or Under-Hangmen, were Drunk. They had forgotten the Pitch, Oil, Rosin, and other things ; and at the last moment they had to be sent for to the neighbouring Grocers'. But these Shop-keepers declared, out of humanity, that they had them not ; whereupon Guards and Exempts were sent, who searched their Stores, and seized what was wanted in the King's Name. Then the Fiendish Show began. I can hear the miserable man's Shrieks as I sit writing this now.——But no more.

So strong is our Human Frame, that the great strong Brewer's Horses, although Dragged and Whipped this way and t'other, could not pull his limbs Asunder. So the Surgeons were obliged to sever the great Sinews with Knives, and then the Horses managed it, somehow.

Note.—When the Horses were Lashed, to make 'em pull Lustily, the Fine Ladies at the windows fluttered their Fans, and, in their sweet little Court Lingo, cried out compassionately, " *Oh, les pauv' Zevaux !*"—— "Oh, the poor Dobbins !" They didn't say any thing about a poor Damiens.

Note.—Also, that when they took his Head, to cram it into the Brazier, and burn it with the rest of his Members, they found that his Hair, which when he was arrested was of a Dark Brown, had turned quite White.

This Story is Naked Truth, and it was done in the Christian country of France, and in the Year of our Lord Seventeen Hundred and Fifty-Seven. It all fell out because a poor, ignorant, half-crazy Serving-

Man chose to muddle his Head about the Archbishop of Paris and his Billets of Confession, and because he would not go to a Chirurgeon and be let Blood when Jack Dangerous bade him.

A week after this his Eminence was pleased to send for me into his Cabinet, and told me that he had heard great Accounts from his Secretary of my Parts, Application, and Capacity, and that he designed to restore me to the position of a Gentleman. He asked me if I had a mind for a particular Employment and a Secret Mission; and on my signifying my willingness to embark in such an Undertaking, bade me hold myself in readiness to travel forthwith into Italy.

CHAPTER THE SIXTH.

OF MY SECRET EMPLOYMENT IN THE SERVICE OF THE CARDINAL DE ———.

PARIS was now clearly no place for me; so bidding adieu to my kind Protectress, I made what haste I could to quit the city where I had witnessed, and in some sense been implicated in, so Frightful a Tragedy. There had always been mingled with my Adventurous Temperament a turn for sober Reflection; and I did not fail to Reflect with much seriousness upon the appalling perils from which I had just, by the Mercy of Providence, escaped. Setting altogether on one side the Pretty Sight I should have presented had I been subject to the Hellish Tortures which this poor crazy Wretch Damiens underwent, I justly conceived an extreme Horror for this Fiendish yet frivolous People, who could mingle the twirling of Fans and the sucking of Sugar-plums, with the most excruciating Torments ever inflicted upon a Human Being. At least, so I reasoned to myself; if we English hang and disembowel a Traitor, at least we strangle him first; and though the sentence is Bloodthirsty, the mob would rend 'Squire Ketch in pieces were it known that a Spark of Life remained in the Body of the Patient when the Hangman's Knife touched his Breast; but these Frenchmen have neither Humanity nor Decency, and positively pet and pamper up their Victim in order that he may be the better able to endure the full effects of their infernal Spite.

Not without considerable Misgivings did I undertake my new Employment, the more so as I was both forbidden and ashamed to impart any inkling of its nature to my dear Mistress. Say what you will, no man that has a spark of Honesty remaining in him can have much relish for the calling of a Spy. I tried hard to persuade myself that this was a kind of Diplomatic Employment;

that I was intrusted with Secrets of State; and that by faithfully carrying out my Instructions, I was serving the cause of Civilisation, and in my humble way helping to maintain the Peace of Europe. For in all ages there have been, and in all to come there must be, sober and discreet Persons to act as Emissaries, to inquire into the conditions of the People, and bring back Tidings of the Nakedness or Fertility of the Land. It would never have been known that there was Corn in Egypt, but for the sagacious Investigations of Messengers sent to quest about in the interest of a Famished Community. Nevertheless I admit that, although I spread much such Balsam upon my galled and chafed Conscience, I could not avoid a dismal Distrust that all these Arguments were vain and Sophistical. The words, "Spy, Spy, Spy," haunted me both by day and by night. I saw, in imagination, the Finger of Derision pointed at me, and heard, in spirit, the wagging of the Tongues of Evil-minded Men. The worst of it was, that the occult nature of my

Mission prevented me from loudly proclaiming my Honesty in order to vindicate it against all comers, and glued my Sword to its Scabbard, whence it would otherwise furiously have leapt to avenge the merest Slight put upon me.

His Eminence the Cardinal de —— was pleased to equip me for my Journey in the most munificent Manner.   First he directed me to procure a plentiful stock of Clothes both for travelling and for gala Occasions, not forgetting a couple of good serviceable Rapiers, as well as a Walking-sword, a Dress-foil, and a Hanger, with a pair of Holster Pistols, and two smaller ones of Steel in case of Emergencies.   Also, by his advice, within the lining of my Coat, by the nape of my Neck, just where the bag of my Wig hung, I secreted a neat little Poniard or Dagger.   In a small Emerald Ring, of which he made me a Present, was compactly stowed a quantity of very subtle and potent Poison, sufficient to kill Two Men.   " One never knows what may happen, dear Captain," says his Eminence to me," with his unctuous Smile. " Your Profession is one of sudden Risks, leading sometimes to prospects of painful Inconvenience. If you are brought to such a pass that all your Ingenuity will not enable you to extricate yourself from it, and if you have any rational Objection, say, to being Burnt Alive, or Broken on the Wheel, 'tis always as well to have the means at hand of executing oneself with genteel Tranquillity. Such means you will always carry with you on your Little Finger ; and I can see, by the circumference of the Ring, that 'tis only by Sawing off that it can be got from off your Digit. Poison yourself then, *mio caro*, if you see no other way of getting out of the Scrape ; but pray remember this ; That he who has poison about him, and only enough for one, is an Ass. *Always carry enough for Two.* The immersion of that little finger in a Glass of Wine, and the pressure of a little Spring, would make Hercules so much cold chicken in a Moment. There are times, dear Captain, when you may have to save Half your Potion to kill yourself, but when you may safely lay out the other Half with the view of killing somebody else." A mighty pleasant Way had his Eminence with him ; and his conversation was a kind of Borgia Brocade shot with Machiavelism.

My Despatches and other Secret Documents I was to carry neatly folded and moulded within a Ball of Wax not much larger than a Pill. This again was put into a Comfit-box of Gold, and suspended by a minute but strong Chain of Steel round my Neck.

"In difficult Circumstances," says his Eminence, "you will open that Comfit-box and swallow that little Ball of Wax. I have often thought," he pursued, "that Spies, to be perfect in their Vocation, should first of all be apprenticed to Mountebanks. At the Fair of St. Germain, I have gazed with admiration on the grotesquely bedizened fellows who swallow Swords, Redhot Pokers, and Yards of Ribbon without number, and thought of what invaluable service their Powers of Gullet would be in the rapid and effectual concealment of Documents the which it is expedient to conceal from the eyes of the Vulgar."

Again, in the folds of a silken belt, in the which I was to keep my Letters of Credit and a large unset Diamond, in case I should be pressed for Money in places where there were no Bankers,—for Diamonds are convertible into Cash from one end of the World to the other, except among the Cannibals,—in this Belt was a little Scrap of Parchment secured between two squares of Glass, and bearing an Inscription in minute characters, which I was unable to decipher. I have the Scrap of Parchment by me yet, and have shown it to Doctor Dubiety, who is a very learned man; but even he is puzzled with it; and beyond opining that the characters are either Arabic or Sanscrit, cannot give me any information regarding their Purport.

" This Parchment," observed the Cardinal when he delivered it to me, " will be of no service to you with Civil or Military Governors, and it will be well for you not to show it to carnal-minded Men; but if ever you get into difficulties with Holy Mother Church—I speak not of Heretic Communions—you may produce it at once, and it will be sure to deliver you from those Fiery Furnaces and the Jaws of those Devouring Dragons of whom the said Holy Mother Church is sometimes forced (through the perversity of Mankind) to make use."

Finally, this same Belt contained a curious Contrivance, by means of a piece of Vellum perforated in divers places, for deciphering the Letters I might receive from his Eminence or his agents. On placing the Vellum over the Letter sent, the words intended to meet the eyes of the recipient, and none other, would appear through the incisions made; while, the Vellum removed, the body of the Epistle would read like the veriest Balderdash. This the French call a *chiffre à grille*, and 'tis much used in their secret Diplomatic Affairs. The best of it is, that when the two Parties who wish to correspond have once settled where the incisions are to be, and have each gotten their *grille*, or Peephole Vellum, no human being can, under ten thousand combinations of letters, and years of toilsome labour, decipher what is meant to be expressed, or Weed out the few Words of Meaning from the mass of surrounding Rubbish.

I bade his Eminence farewell, having the honour to be admitted to his *petit lever*, the felicity to kiss his hand and receive his Benediction, and the distinction of being conducted down the Back Stairs by his Maître d'Hôtel, and let out by a Side Door in the Garden-wall of his Mansion. A close Chariot took me one morning in the Spring of '58 to the Barrière de Lyon, and there I found a Chaise and Post-horses, and was soon on my road to the South, with three hundred Louis in Gold in my Valise, and a Letter of Credit for any sum under five hundred at a time, I liked to draw, in my Waist-belt. I was Richer in Purse and more bravely Dressed than ever I had been in my life, and travelled under the name of the Chevalier Escarbotin; but I was a Spy, and in mine own eyes I was the Meanest of the Mean.

A happy Mercurial Temper and cheerful Flow of Spirits soon, however, revived within me; and, ere Ten Leagues of my Journey were over, the Chevalier Escarbotin became once more to himself Jack Dangerous. "I will work the Mine of my Manhood," I cried out in the Chaise, "to the last Vein of the Ore. *Vive la Joie!*" Yet in my innermost heart did I wish myself once more with Captain Blokes as the daring Supercargo of the dear old *Marquis,* or else a Peaceful Merchant at Amsterdam, giving good advice to the Rogues and Sluts in the Rasphuys. O Mr. Vandepeereboom, Mr. Vandepeereboom!

Six days after my departure from Paris, I embarked from Marseille on board a Tartane bound for Genoa. We had fine sailing for about three days, till by contrary winds we were driven into San Remo, a pretty Seaport belonging to the Genoese. This abounds so much with Oranges, Lemons,

and other Delicious Fruit, that it is called
the Paradise of Italy. So on to Genoa,
where the Beggars live in Palaces cheek by
jowl with the Nobles, who are well-nigh as
beggarly as they; and the Houses are as
lofty as any in Europe, and the Streets
between them as dark and narrow as Adam
and Eve Court in the Strand. The Suburb
called San Pietro d'Arena very pretty, and
full of commodious Villas. There are thirty
Parish Churches, and at San Lorenzo they
show a large Dish made out of One
Emerald, which they say was given to King
Solomon by the Queen of Sheba. The
Genoese are a cunning and industrious
People, with a great gusto for the Arts, but
terrible Thieves. The Government a Re-
public, headed by a Doge, that is chosen
every two years from among the Nobility,
and must be a Genoese, at least Fifty years
of age, and no Byblow. He cannot so much
as lie One Night out of the City, without
leave had from the Senate. When he is
elected, they place a Crown of Gold on his

Head, and a Sceptre in his Hand.   His.
Robes are of Crimson Velvet, and he has
the title of Serenity.

Here I did business with several Persons
of Consideration; the Senators B—c—i and
Della G——, the rich Banker L——, and
Monsignore the Archprelate X——.   So by
Cortona, where there is a strong Castle on
a Hill, to Pavia, an old decaying City on
the River Tessin, which is so rapid that
Bishop Burnet says he ran down the Stream
thirty miles in three hours by the help of
one Rower only.   This may be, or t'other
way; but I own to placing very little faith
in the veracity of these Cat-in-Pan Revolu-
tion Bishops.   Here (at Pavy) is a Brass
Statue of Marcus Antoninus on Horseback;
though the Pavians will have it to be
Charles the Fifth, and others declare it to
be Constantine the Great.

After two days here, waiting for Despatches from his Eminence, which came at
last in the False Bottom of a Jar of Nar-
bonne Honey, and I answering by a Billet
discreetly buried in the recesses of a large

Bologna Sausage, I posted to Milan, through a fertile and delicious country, which some call the Garden of Italy. A broad, clean place, with spacious Streets ; but the Wine and Maccaroni not half so good as at Genoa. The Cathedral full of Relics, some of which run up as high as Abraham. In the Ambrosian Library are a power of Books, and, what is more curious, the Dried *Heads* of several Learned Men—amongst others, that of our Bishop Fisher, whom King Harry the Eighth put to death for not acknowledging his Supremacy. About two miles from hence is a Curiosity, in the shape of a Building, where, if you fire off a Pistol, the Sound returns about Fifty times. 'Tis done, they told me, by two Parallel Walls of a considerable length, which reverberate the Sound to each other till the undulation is quite spent. The which, being so informed, I was as wise concerning the Echo as I had been before.

It was my Design to have proceeded from Milan either to Venice or to the famous Capital City of Rome ; but Instructions from his Eminence forced me to retrace my steps, and at Genoa I embarked for Naples. This is a very handsome place, but villanously Dirty, and governed in a most Despotic Manner. Nearly all the Corn Country round about belongs to the Jesuits, who make a pretty Penny by it. The taxes very high, and laid on Wine, Meat, Oil, and other Necessaries of Life ; indeed on every thing eatable except Fruit and Fowls, which you may buy for a Song. All Foreigners who have here purchased Estates are loaded with Extraordinary Taxes and Impositions. The City is remarkable for its Silk Stockings, Waistcoats, Breeches, and Caps ; Soap, Perfume, and Snuff-boxes. They cool their Wine with Snow, which they get out of pits dug in the Mountain-sides. Near here, too, is a Burning Mountain they call Vesuvio. It may be mighty curious, but 'tis as great a Nuisance and Perpetual Alarm to the peaceable Inhabitants of Naples as a Powder Magazine. Very often this Vesuvio gives itself up to hideous Bellowing, causing the Windows, nay the very Houses, in Naples to Shake, and then it vomits forth vast Quantities of melted Stuff, which streams down the Mountain-sides like a pot boiling over. Sometimes it darkens the Sun with Smoke, causing a kind of Eclipse; then a Pillar of Black Smoke will start up to a prodigious Height in the air, and the next morning you will find the Court and Terrace of your House, be it ten miles away, all strewn with Fine Ashes from Vesuvio.

CHAPTER THE SEVENTH.

I FALL INTO THE HANDS OF RECREANT PAYNIMS, AND AM REDUCED TO A STATE OF MISERABLE SLAVERY.

I THINK I should have been much better off, if, stopping at Naples, I had fallen into the blazing Crater of Vesuvio, and have cast up again into the air in the shape of Red-Hot Ashes.   I think it would have been better for me to be Bitten by the Tarantula Spider (which is about the size of a small Nutmeg, and when it bites a person throws him into all kinds of Tumblings, Anger, Fear, Weeping, Crazy Talk, and Wild Actions, accompanied by a kind of Bedlam Gambado), than to have gone upon the pretty Dance I was destined to Lead.   However, there was no disobeying the commands of his Eminence, who, in his Smooth Italian way, told me at Paris that those of his Servants who did not attend to his Behests, were much subject to dying Suddenly after Supper; and so, Willy-nilly, I sped upon my Dark Errand.

Business now took me to Venice. This is a very grand City, both for the Magnificence of its Nobles and the Extent of its Commerce. The Doge is only a Sumptuous kind of Puppet, the Real Government being vested in the Seignory, or Council of Ten, that carry matters with a very High Hand, but, on the whole, give Satisfaction both to the Quality and the Common. Here are numbers of Priests of a very Free Life and Conversation, and swarms of Monks that are notorious Evil-doers; for during the Carnival (a very famous one here) they wear Masks, sing upon Stages, and fall into many other Practices unbecoming their Profession. The Venetian Nuns are the merriest in all Europe, and have a not much better Repute than the Monks, many of them being the Daughters of the Nobility, who dispose of 'em in this manner to save the Charges of keeping 'em at home. They wear no Veils; have their Necks uncovered; and receive the Addresses of Suitors at the Grates of their Parlours. The Patriarch did indeed at one time essay to Reform the abuses that had crept into the Nunneries; but the Ladies of San Giacomo, with whom he began, told him plainly that they were Noble Venetians, and scorned his Regulations. Thereupon he attempted to shut up their House, which so provoked 'em that they were going to set Fire to it; but the Senate interposing, commanded the Patriarch to desist, and these Merry Maidens had full liberty to resume their Madcap Pranks.

Here they make excellent fine Drinking-glasses and Mirrors; likewise Gold and Silver Stuffs, Turpentine, Cream of Tartar, and other articles. The Streets mostly with Water running thro' 'em, like unto Rotterdam, all going to and fro done in Boats called Gondoles,—a dismal, Hearse-looking kind of Wherry, with a prow like the head of a Bass-Viol, and rowed, or rather shoved along with a Pole by a Mad, Ragged Fellow, that bawls out verses from Tasso, one of their Poets, as he plies his Oar. The great Sight at Venice, after the Grand Canal and St. Mark's Place, is the Carnival, which begins on Twelfth Day, and holds all Lent. The Diversion of the Venetians is now all for Masquerading. Under a Disguise, they break through their Natural Gravity, and fall heartily into all the Follies and Extravagances of these occasions. With Operas, Plays, and Gaming-Houses, they seem to forget all Habits, Customs, and Laws; lay aside all cares of Business, and swamp all Distinctions of Rank. This practice of Masking gives rise to a variety of Love Adventures, of which the less said the better; for the Venetian Bona Robas, or Corteggiane, as they call 'em now, are a most Artful Generation. The pursuit of Amours is often accompanied by Broils and Bloodshed; and Fiery Temper is not confined to the Men, but often breaks out in the Weaker Sex; an instance of which I saw one day in St. Mark's Place, where two Fine Women, Masked, that were Rivals for the favour of the 'same Gallant, happening to meet, and by some means knowing one

another, they fell out, went to Cuffs, tore off
each other's Mask, and at last drew Knives
out of their pockets, with which they Fought
so seriously, that one of them was left for
Dead upon the Spot.

Another Frolic of the Carnival is Gaming,
which is commonly in Noblemen's Houses,
where there are Tables for that purpose in
ten or twelve Rooms on a floor, and seldom
without abundance of Company, who are all
Masked, and observe a profound Silence.
Here one meets Ladies of Pleasure cheek by
jowl with Ladies of Quality, who, under the
protection of a convenient piece of Black
Satin or Velvet, are allowed to enjoy the
entertainments of the Season ; but are generally attended either by the Husband or his
Spies, who keep a watchful eye on their
Behaviour.   Besides these Gaming-Rooms,
there are others, where Sweetmeats, Wine,
Lemonade, and other Refreshments may be
purchased, the Haughty Nobility of Venice
not disdaining to turn Tavern-keepers at
this season of the year.   Here it is usual for
Gentlemen to address the Ladies and employ

their wit and raillery ; but they must take care to keep within the bounds of Politeness, or they may draw upon themselves the Resentment of the Husbands, who seldom put up with an Affront of this kind, though perhaps only imaginary, without exacting a severe Satisfaction. For the Common People there are Jugglers, Rope-dancers, Fortune-tellers, and other Buffoons, who have stages in the Square of St. Mark, where, at all times during the Carnival, 'tis almost impossible to pass along, owing to the crowd of Masqueraders. Bull Baitings, Races of Gondoles, and other Amusements, too tedious to enumerate, also take place. But among the several Shows which attract the eyes of the Populace, I cannot forbear describing one which is remarkable for its oddity, and perhaps peculiar to the Venetians. A number of Men, by the help of Poles laid across each other's Shoulders, build themselves up almost as children do Cards—four or five Rows of 'em standing one above the other, and lessening as they advance in height, till at last a little Boy forms the

Top, or Point, of the Structure. After they have stood in this manner, to be gazed at, some time, the Boy leaps down into the arms of people appointed to catch him at the Bottom; the rest follow his example; and so the whole Pile falls to Pieces.

The Nobility of Venice are remarkable for their Persons as well as for their Polite Behaviour, and have a great deal of Gravity and Wisdom in their Countenances. They wear a light Cap with a kind of black Fringe, and a long black Gown of Paduan Cloth, as their Laws require; though the English have found means to introduce their Manufactures among 'em. Underneath these Gowns they have suits of Silk; and are extremely neat as to their Shoes and Stockings. Their Perukes are long, full-bottomed, and very well Powdered; and they usually carry their Caps in their Hands. The Women very well shaped, though they endeavour to improve their Complexions with Washes and Paint. These of Quality wear such high-heeled Shoes, that they can scarce walk without having two people to support them. In matters of Religion (though their worship is as pompous as Gold and Jewels can make it) the Venetians are very Easy and Unconcerned; and neither Pope nor Inquisition is thought much of in the Dominions of the Seignory. For Music in their Churches they have a perfect Passion. The City is well furnished with Necessaries; but the want of Cellarage makes all the Wine sour. The Inhabitants are of a Fresh Complexion, and not much troubled with Coughs; which is strange, they having so much Water about 'em. They begin their day at Sunset, and count one . o'clock an hour after, and so on to twenty-four; which is likewise a Custom, I believe, among the Chineses.

They bury their Dead within the Four-and-Twenty Hours, and sometimes sooner. The Funerals of Persons of Quality are performed with great Pomp and Solemnity; and the deceased are carried to the Place of Interment with their Faces bare. Whilst I was in Venice, their Patriarch (who is a kind of Independent Pontiff in his own

way ; for, as I have said, they reckon but
little of his Holiness here) died, and was
buried with this Ceremony.   He was carried
in one of his own Coaches, by night, to St.
Mark's Church, which was all hung with
Black for the occasion ; and next day the
Corpse was laid on a Bed in the very middle
of the Church, dressed in the Sacerdotal
Habit, with the Head towards the Choir,
and his Tiara, or Mitre, lying at the feet.
At each corner of the bed stood a *valet de
chambre*, holding a Banner of Black Taffety,
with the Arms of the Deceased.   A hundred
large Wax. Tapers were placed in Candle-
sticks round the bed, and High Mass was
sung ; the Sopranos very beautiful.   After
Mass was over, all retired ; but the Body
lay exposed till evening, when it was stripped
of its Vestments (for though a very Gorgeous
people, they are Economical in their ways),
and put into a Leaden Coffin, enclosed in
another of Cypress, and was then let down
into the Grave.   'Tis not usual with the
Relations to attend the Funeral, which they
look upon as a Barbarous Custom.   But

they wear Mourning longer and more regularly than in many other countries. A woman in a Mourning Habit appears Black from Head to Foot, not the least Bit of Linen being to be seen.

The nature of my Employment now brought me into intimate Commerce with Monsieur B——, a French Merchant of Lyons, who treated me with extraordinary Civility, and made great Offers of being of Assistance to me in my Voyage to Constantinople, whither I was now Bound. This Gentleman, by means of the French Ambassador at the Porte, had gotten a Firman, or passport, to enable him to Travel to that City, and with a proper number of Attendants, through any part of the Turkish Dominions. As 'tis inconvenient and dangerous Voyaging though the territories of the Great Turk without such a Protection, nothing could be more Agreeable than the offer he made me of his Company, the more so as his Eminence had enjoined me to keep a Strict Watch upon every thing that M. B—— said or did. He had designed to reach Constantinople by Land through Bosnia, Servia, Bulgaria, and Roumania; yet, in compliance with my Inclination (I wish my Inclination had been at the Deuce), which was all for a Sea Passage, he consented to embark on board a Vessel bound to Candia and other Islands of the Archipelago, from which we were to procure a Passage to the Capital of the Ottoman Empire. What made this Gentleman's Society more acceptable, was his thorough Knowledge of the Trade of the Levant, and the Genius and Temper of the People. Thus, he informed me of the Method of Dealing with Jews, Armenians, and Greeks; of the Eastern manner of travelling in Caravans, and the necessary precautions against such Accidents as are mostly fatal to Strangers; and instructed me in the Art of concealing Things of Value,—although I think I too could have given him a lesson in that Device,—and avoiding those Snares which Governors, Military Officers, and Petty Princes make use of in order to plunder Travellers and Merchants. Under these favourable Auspices, we embarked, in the Autumn of '37, on board a Trading Vessel called the *San Marco*, bound for Candia, but first for Malta, so famous for its Order of Knights. A fine Gale at North-West carried us pleasantly down the Gulf of Venice, or Adriatic Sea; and on the fifth day we came in sight of Otranto, a Town destroyed by the Turks nigh Three Hundred years ago, since which time it has hardly regained its Ancient Lustre, but at present well Fortified, and defended by a High Castle, which I have heard the Honourable Mr. Walpole, a Fine, Lardy-Dardy, Maccaroni Gentleman, that lives at a place called Strawberry Hill, by Twitnam, in England, has written a silly Romantic Tale about. So we got clear of the Gulf of Venice, and in three days more, after making Cape Passaro in Sicily, entered the Haven of Malta.

This is an Island that lies between Sicily and the Coast of Africa, and is of an Egg-shaped figure, about twenty miles long and twelve broad. The City of Malta is divided into three parts, which are properly so many

Rocks jutting out into the Sea, with large Harbours between them. That called Valetta, in honour of the Grand Master who so gallantly defended the place against the Turks, is extremely well Fortified, and also defended by a Castle, held to be impregnable. The City contains about Two Thousand Houses, well built with white Stone, and Flat-roofed, surrounded by Rails and Balusters. On t'other side of the Harbour is another City, formerly called Il Borgo, or the Borough, but now named Città Vittoriosa, alluding to the terrible Mauling the Turks got here in 1566. St. John's Church very handsome, and on one side of it a fine Piazza, with a Fountain in the corner. Here are all the Tombs of the Grand Masters, and a great many Flags taken from the Turks. The Right Hand of St. John Baptist, wanting but Two Fingers, shown here for Money, with many other Relics and Ornaments. The Grand Master lives in a magnificent Palace; and close by is an Arsenal, with Arms for Thirty Thousand Men.

The Treasury is a very stately Edifice; but what gives the highest Idea of the Charity of this illustrious Order is their noble Hospital, where all the Sick are received and provided for with the utmost Care. The Rooms are large and commodious, and in each of them there are but two Patients. Their Diet is brought to them in rich Silver Plate by the Knights themselves, who are obliged to this attendance by their Constitutions; and such an exact Decorum is observed, and every thing performed with such Magnificence, that it raises the astonishment of Strangers.

But if there be Charity and Benevolence for the Christian Sick, there is little Mercy shown towards Infidels and Miscreants. The Prison for the Slaves is an enormous Building, with a Colonnade running round it, and capable of lodging three or four Thousand of those Unhappy People. There are seldom less than Two Thousand in the House, except when the Galleys of the Order are at Sea upon some Expedition. Then the poor Wretches are Chained, Night and Day, to the Oar ; but when on Shore they have only a small Lock on their Ankles, like the slaves at Leghorn, and are permitted to go to any part of the Island, from which they have seldom an opportunity of making their Escape.

The Knights of the Order of St. John of Jerusalem, commonly called Knights of Malta, after removing from Jerusalem to Magrath, from thence to Acre, and thence to Rhodes, were expelled from that Island by the Sultan Solyman, having an Army of Three Hundred Thousand Men. The Knights retired, first to Candia, and then to Sicily ; but at last the Emperor Charles the Fifth gave 'em the Island of Malta, which they hold to this day. They formerly consisted of Eight Languages or Tongues, according to their Different Nations, viz. those of Provence, Auvergne, France, Italy, Arragon, Germany, Castile, and England ; but this last one has been extinct since our Harry the Eighth's time, and what English Knights there be who are Papists are forced to find their Tongue where they can. Each of the

Languages has its Chiefs, who are also called Pillars and Grand Crosses, being distinguished by a large White Cross 'broidered on their Breasts. The Seven Languages have their respective Colleges and Halls in Malta, the Head of each House being called the Grand Prior of his Nation ; and to each belongs a certain number of his Commanderies. The Knights, at their entrance into the Order, must prove their Legitimacy, as well as Nobility, by four Descents, and are termed Chevaliers by Right. Those who are raised to the rank of Nobles, for some Valiant Exploit, are called Chevaliers by Favour. None are admitted by the Statutes of the Order under the age of Sixteen ; but some are received from their very Infancy on paying a large Sum of Money, or by Dispensation from the Pope. All the Knights oblige themselves to Celibacy, which does not hinder their leading very Disorderly Lives ; and indeed Malta is full of Loose Cattle of all kinds. When they are Professed, a Carpet is spread on the Ground, on which is set a Piece of Bread, a Cup of Water, and a Naked Blade; and they are told, "This is what Religion gives you. You must procure yourself the rest with your Sword." The which they do, to a pretty considerable Tune, by spoiling of the Turks. After they make their Vows, they wear a White Cross or Star, with Eight Points, over their Cloaks or Coats, on the Left Side, which is the proper Badge of their Order, the Golden Maltese Cross being only an Ornament. The ordinary Habit of the Grand Master is a kind of Cassock, open before, and tied about him with a Girdle, at which hangs a Purse, alluding to the Charitable ends of their Order;—but 'tis not to be denied that they have grown very Proud, and Live, many of 'em, in as Shameful Luxury as the Prince Bishops of Germany. Over his Cassock the Grand Master wears a Velvet Gown or Cloak when he goes to Church on Solemn Festivals. He is addressed under the Title of Eminence by all the Knights; but his Subjects of Malta, and the Neighbouring Islands, style him Your Highness. As Sovereign, he coins Money, pardons Criminals, and bestows the places of Grand Priors, Bailiffs, &c. ; but in most cases of importance is obliged to seek the advice of his Council, so that he is not wholly Absolute. The Ecclesiastics proper of the Order—for the rest are but Military Monks, that do a great deal more Fighting' than Praying, and savour much more of the Camp than of the Convent—are Chaplains, Monastic Clerks, and Deacons. They likewise wear a White Cross, partake of the Privileges of the Institution, and are great Rascals.

'Tis well known that the Knights of Malta are destined to the Profession of Arms for the Defence of the Christian Faith, and the Protection of Pilgrims of all Nations. It is to be observed, that there are also Female Hospitallers of the Order of St. John, sometimes called Chevalières, or She-Knights, of equal Antiquity with the Knights, whose business it is to take care of the Women Pilgrims in a Hospital apart from that of the Men. As the Order look upon the Turks as the Great Enemies of Christianity, they think themselves obliged to be in a state of perpetual Hostility with that people, and, for Centuries, have never so much as signed the preliminaries of a Peace with 'em. They have performed innumerable and astonishing exploits against their much-hated Enemies, the Insolence of whose Rovers they continue to Restrain and Chastise, except when the Rovers, as sometimes happens, get the better of 'em. They have Seven Galleys belonging to the Order, each of which carries Five Hundred Men, and as many Wretches in Fetters tugging away at the Oar, for Dear Life. Every one of these Galleys mounts Sixteen Pieces of Heavy Artillery; and besides these they fit out a great many Private Ships, by license from the Grand Master, to cruise up and down among the Turks, doing great Havoc, and thereby growing very Rich. Thus it will be plain to the Reader that a Knight of Malta is a kind of Medley of Seaman, Swashbuckler, and Saint—Admiral Benbow, Field-Marshal Wade, and Friar Tuck all rolled up into one.

I did become acquainted with one of

these Holy Roystering Cavalieros, by the name of Don Ercolo Amadeo Sparafucile di San Lorenzo, that was a perfect Model of all these Characteristics. He Confessed with almost as great regularity as he Sinned. The Chaplains must have held him as one of the heartiest of Penitents; for he never came back from a Cruise without a whole Sackful of Misdeeds, and straightway hied him to St. John's Church, to fling his Sinful Ballast overboard and lighten ship. How he swore! I never heard a man take the entrails of Alexander the Great in vain before; but this was an ordinary expletive with Don Ercolo. He belonged to the Italian Language, though I suspected he had a dash of the Spanish in him; and many a Gay Bout over the choicest of Wines have I had with him at his Inn, as their College-halls are sometimes called. He could drink like a Fish, and fight like a Paladin. He was a good Practical Sailor and Master of Navigation; Rode with ease and dexterity; and was a Proficient in that most difficult trick of the *Manège*, that of riding a horse *en Biais,* as the French term it, and of which our Newcastle has learnedly treated; was an admirable Performer on the Guitar and Viol di Gamba; Sung very sweetly; Fenced exquisitely; must have been in his Youth (he was now about Sixty, and his Hair was grizzled grey) as Beautiful as a Woman, as Graceful as my Sweet Protectress Lilias, as Brave as the Cid, and as Cruel as Pedro of Spain. As·it is so long ago, and the Principal Parties in the Affair are all Dead, I don't mind disclosing that my Instructions from his Eminence the Cardinal were to Buy the Cavaliere di San Lorenzo at any Price. I told him so plainly over a Flask of Right Alicant, at a little Feast I had made for him in return for his many Hospitalities, and gave him to understand that he had but to say the word, and Scroppa, the great Goldsmith of Strada Reale, would be glad to cash his Draft for any Sum under Fifty Thousand Ducats. For his Eminence wanted the Cavaliere to be a Friend of France, and France at that time thought that she very much wanted the Island of Malta.

Don Ercolo was not in the least angry; only, he Laughed in my Face.

"Chevalier Escarbotin," he said gaily, "you have mistaken your man. Tell his Eminence the Cardinal de —— that he may go and hang himself. I am not to be bought. I am Rich to Two Hundred and Fifty Thousand ounces of Gold, all got out of spoiling the Infidels. When I die, I shall leave half to the Order, and half to the families of certain Poor Women Creatures whom I have wronged, and who are Dead."

I said, to appease him, that I was but Joking.

"Ta, ta, ta!" retorts he. "I know your Trade well enough. I have been too much among men not to be able to scent out a Spy. But you are a very Jovial Fellow, Escarbotin; and I don't care what you are, so long as you are not a Turk, which, by the way, I don't think you would mind turning."

"O, Signore Cavaliere!"——I began to ex-
postulate.

"What does it matter?" quoth Don
Ercolo. "Does it matter anything at all?
Perhaps some of these days, when I am tired
of the Eight Points, I shall take the Turban
myself."

"A Renegado!" I cried.

"Many a brave Gentleman has turned
Renegado ere this," answered he. "Next to
the pleasure of Fighting the Turks, I should
esteem the condition of being a Turk myself,
and fighting against the Order of Malta.
But I forgot. You are a Lutheran; although
how you came to be a Protestant, with that
name of Escarbotin, I can't make out."

I murmured something about belonging
to the Reformed Church at Geneva; although
I forgot that they were mostly Calvinists
there, not Lutherans. But of this Don Ercolo
took little notice, and went on.

"When you write to the Cardinal, tell him
that Ercolo Amadeo Sparafucile di San Lorenzo is not to be purchased. The sly old
Fox! He knows I have great influence with

my Uncle the Grand Master. Tell him that I am very much obliged to him for his Offer, and thank him for old Acquaintance' sake. Nay; I believe I am some kind of Kinsman of his Eminence, on the Mother's side. But assure him that I am not in the least Angry with him. If I were Poor, I should probably accept his Offer; but none of the Poor Knights of our Order are worth Buying. It matters little to me whether France, or Spain, or even Heretic England gets hold of this scorching Rock, with its Swarms of Hussies and Rascals; only I prefer amusing myself, and fighting the Turks, to meddling in Politics, and running the risk of a life-long dungeon in the Castle of St. Elmo."

There was a long Silence after this, and he seemed plunged in profound Meditation. Suddenly he fills a Cup with Wine, drains it, and, in his old careless manner, says to me,

" Tell him this—be sure to tell him, lest he should be at the trouble of sending Emissaries to Poison me—I have the best Antidote of any in the Levant, and shall take three drops of it after every Bite and Sup for Six Months to come. Not that I dread you. All Spy as you are, you still look like an Honest Fellow. *You* would not poison an old Friend, would you, Little JACK DANGEROUS?"

I started to my feet, and stared at the grizzled, handsome Knight in blank amazement. We had been conversing in the French tongue; but the latter part of his Speech he had uttered in mine own English, and with a faultless accent. Moreover, where before had I heard that Voice, had I seen that Face? My Memory rolled back over the hills and valleys of years; but the Mountains were too high, and the Recesses behind them inaccessible without Mental Climbing, for which I was not prepared.

"Little Jack Dangerous," continued the grizzled Knight, "where have you been these Seven-and-thirty Years? When I knew you first, you were but a poor little Runaway Schoolboy, and I was a Tearing Fellow in the Flush and Pride of my hot Youth."

"A Runaway Schoolboy!" I stammered.

"Ay! had you not fled from the Tyranny of one Gnawbit?"

"I remember Gnawbit well," I answered, with a shudder.

"Do you remember Charlwood Chase, and the Blacks that were wont to kill Venison there?"

"I do."

"And Mother Drum, and Cicely, and Jowler, and the Night Attack, and how near you were being hanged? Do you remember Captain NIGHT?"

A Light broke in upon me. I recognised my earliest Protector. I seized his Hand. I was fairly blubbering, and would have rushed into his Arms; but there was something Cold and Haughty in his Manner that repulsed me.

"'Tis well," he said. "I am a Knight of the most Illustrious Order of St. John of Jerusalem, and an Italian Cavalier of Degree. You——"

"I am a Spy," I cried out half-sobbing. "What was I to do? My Malignant Fate hath ever been against me.   I am despicable in your Eyes, but not so despicable as I am in mine own."

"There, there," he cries out, very placably. "There's no great harm done, and there's much of a muchness between us.   When you first came across me, was I not stealing the King's Deer in Charlwood Chase, besides being in trouble—I don't mind owning to you now — on account of King James? 'Twixt you, Jack Dangerous, Flibustier, Saltabadil, and Spy, and Captain Night, now called Don Ercolo et cetera, et cetera di San Lorenzo, and a Knight of Malta, there is not much, perhaps, to choose.   The World hath its strange Ups and Downs, and we must e'en make the best of them.   Sit you down, Jack Dangerous, and we will have t'other Flask."

We had t'other Flask, and very good Wine it was; and for the rest of the time I remained in Malta, Don Ercolo continued to be my Fast Friend, even as he had been in my Youth.   And yet 'twas mainly through his Instrumentality that I quitted the Island;

for he sent his Page to me with a Letter, written in our own dear English Tongue, in the which he instantly desired me, as I valued my Life and the Interests of my Employers, to put the Broad Seas between myself and the Grand Master; for that an Inkling of my Errand had got wind, and that the Party unfavourable to France being then uppermost, I ran immediate risk of being cast into a Dungeon, if not Hanged. For this Reason, said Don Ercolo, he must forbear any further Commerce with me (not wishing to draw Suspicion on himself, for the Knights are very jealous in Political Affairs); but he assured me of his continued Friendship, and desired if I stood in Need of any Funds for my Journey, to inform the Page, that he might furnish me secretly with what Gold I needed. But I wanted nothing in this way, having ample Credits; so making up my Valises with all convenient Speed, the Chevalier Escarbotin bade adieu to Malta.

I took a passage in a Speronare that was bound to Candia, where I hoped to find some Trading Vessel of heavier Burden to take me to Constantinople. The Mediterranean Sea here very beautiful, and delightful to see the Dolphins, Tunnies, and other Fish, that frequently leapt out of the Water, and followed our Ship in great Numbers. Also a Waterspout, which is a Phenomenon very well known to Seamen in the Levant Trade, and reckoned very dangerous. It looked mighty Fierce and Terrific; and our Sailors, to conjure it away, had recourse to the Superstitious Devices of cutting the air with a Black-Handled Knife, and reading the First Chapter of St. John's Gospel, accounted of great Efficacy in dispersing these Spouts.

Woe is me! After Six Days' most pleasant Sailing, and after doubling Cape Spada, and in very sight of Canea (which is the Port of Candia), a strange Sail hove in Sight, gave Chase, came up to us an hour before sundown, and without as much as, By your leave, or With your leave, opened Fire upon us. A Couple of Swingeers from her Double-shotted Guns were a Bellyful for our poor little Speronare, in which there were but Ten

Men and a Boy, Passengers included; and we were fain to submit. Oh, the intolerable Shame and Disgrace! that Jack Dangerous, who had been All Round the World with that Renowned Commander, Captain Blokes, and had Chased, Taken, and Plundered many a good tall ship belonging to the Spaniards,—ay, and had landed on their Main, Spoiled their Cities and Settlements, Toasted their fine Ladies, and held their Chief Governors to Ransom,—should be laid in the Bilboes by a Rascally African Pirate Vessel mounting Nine Guns, and belonging to the most Heathenish, Knavish, and Bloodthirsty Town of Algiers. My Gall works now to think of it; but Force was against us, and the Disaster was not to be helped. I was in such a Mad Rage as to be near Braining the Captain of the Speronare with a Marline-Spike, and would have assuredly blown out the Brains of the first Moor that boarded us, had not the Italian Captain and his Mate seized each one of my arms, and by Main Force wrested my Weapons from me. And in this (though hotly enraged with 'em at first, and calling them all kinds of Abusive Epithets) I think they acted less like Traitors than like Persons of Sense and Discretion; for what were we Ten (and the Boy) against full Fifty powerful Devils, all armed to the Teeth, and who would assuredly have cut all our Throats had we shown the least Resistance?

So they had their Will of us, and we were all made Prisoners, preparatory to undergoing the worse Fate of Slaves. Vain now, indeed, were all his Eminence's Secret Precautions about the Concealment of Missives; for these Rascal Moors made no more ado, but stripped us of every Rag of Clothing, ripping up the Seams thereof, and examining our very Hair, in quest of Gold and Jewels. The Boatswain, however, that was appointed to search me, after taking from me all my Stock of Money, which was Considerable, returned to me the famous Bit of Parchment between the Glasses, which was to bear me Harmless against the Claws of Holy Mother Church if she happened to turn Tiger-Cat; for these Mahometans have a profound respect for Charms and Amulets, and very like he took this for one, which could be no good to him, an Infidel, but might serve a Frank at a pinch. There was another Article, too, which he restored to me, after Examination, and of which I have hitherto made no mention. What was this but a little Portrait of my Beloved Protectress, which I carried with me next my Heart? Not that I had ever ventured to be so bold as to Ask her for such a pledge, or that she had been complaisant enough to give it me ; but while I was in Paris there had been limned by the great French Painter, Monsieur Boucher, a Picture of one of the Opera Ballets, not Orpheus's Story, but something out of Homer's Poetry,—*Ulysse chez Alcinous*, I think 'twas called,—and this Picture contained very Life-like Effigies of all the Dancers that stood in the front rank, of whom my sweet Mistress Lilias was one. From this an Engraving in the Line Manner was made, which was put forth by the Print-sellers just before I left Paris ; and I declare I gave a Louis d'Or, and Ten Livres, Twelve

Sols, for a Copy, and cutting out the Pictured Head of my Protectress with a sharp Penknife, had it pasted down and framed in a Golden Locket.   When the Boatswain saw this, he Grinned, till the Turban round his tawny Head might have been taken for a Horse-collar.   He wrenched the Portrait out of its Frame, and put the Gold among the heap of Plunder that was gathered, for after division, on the Deck, and was then about to throw the dear Bit of Paper into the Sea,— for these Moors think it Sinful to portray the Human Countenance in any way,—but I besought him so Earnestly, both by Signs and supplicatory Gestures, and even, I believe, Tears, to restore it to me, that he desisted ; and putting his Finger to his Lips, as a Hint that I was not to reveal his Clemency to his Commander, gave me back my precious Portrait.   He would have, however, the fine Chain I wore round my Neck ; so I was fain to make an Opening between the two Sheets of Glass that covered my Amulet, and push in the Portrait, face downwards ; and the two together I hung to a bit of slender Lanyard. But all my brave Clothes were taken from me, and in an Hour after my Capture I was Bare-footed, and with no other Apparel than a Ragged Shirt and a Pair of Drawers of Canvas. To this Accoutrement was speedily added about Twenty-one Pounds of Fetters on the Wrists and Ankles; and then I, and the Captain, and the Mate, and the Men, and the Boy, were put into a Boat and taken on board the Algerine, where we were flung into the Hold, and had nothing better to eat for many days than Mouldy Biscuit and Bilge-Water. The Cargo of the Speronare was mostly Crockery-ware and Household Stuff, for the use of the Candiotes; and the Moors would not be at the trouble of Removing, so they Scuttled her, and bore away to the Norrard.

Item.—I swallowed my Despatches; but the Moors got hold of my Letters of Credit and my Cipher.

CHAPTER THE EIGHTH.

AFTER MANY SURPRISING VICISSITUDES, J. DANGEROUS BECOMES BESTUSCHID BASHAW.

So we were all taken into Algiers. 'Tis called " The Warlike " by that proud People, the Turks ; but with much more Reason, I think, should it be named " The Thievish." Out upon the Robbers' Den! This most abominable Place, which has, during so many Ages, braved the Resentment of the most powerful Princes of Christendom, is said to contain above 100,000 Mahometans,—among them not above Thirty Renegadoes,—15,000 Jews, and 4000 Christian Slaves. 'Tis full of Mosques and other Heathenish places of Worship, and is strongly Fortified, both towards the Sea and the Land. The Ship that took us was a Brigantine ; and they have nigh a Hundred of 'em (besides Row-boats), mounting from Ten to Fifty Guns, with which they ravage the Trade of Europe. There is little within the City that is Curious, save the Dogs, which are very abundant, and very Fierce and Nasty. The Street Bab-Azoun is full of Shops, and Jews dealing in Gems and Goldsmiths' Work. The Hills and Valleys round the City are every where beautified with Gardens and Country Seats, whither the Wealthy Turks retire during the Heats of Summer. Some of the Wild Bedoween Tribes up the country go Bare-headed, binding their Temples only with a Fillet to prevent their hair growing trouble-some. But the Moors and Turks in Algiers wear on the Crowns of their Heads a small Cap of Scarlet Woollen Cloth, that is made at Fez. The Turban is folded round the bottom of these Caps, and by the fashion of the folds you can tell the Soldiers from the Citizens. The Arabs wear a loose Garment called a Hyke, which serves them as a com-plete Dress by Day, and a Bed and Coverlet by Night. 'Tis observable that when the

Moorish Women appear in Public, they
constantly fold themselves so close up in
their Hykes that very little of their Faces
can be seen; but in the Summer Months,
when they retire to their Country Seats,
they walk about with less Caution and
Reserve, and, at the approach of a Stranger,
only let fall their Veils.

What became of the Master and Crew of
the Speronare I know not.   They were but
Weakly Creatures; and I conjecture were
sold off into private Hands and sent up the
country.   Now, although I was past the
Middle Age, and indeed drifting into years,
I was still of Unbowed Stature and great
Strength, and a Personable Fellow, hardened
in the furnace of Danger and Adventure.
This led to my being reserved from the
public Slave-Market for the Dey of Algiers'
own use.   Woe is me, again!   The Distinction profited me little, for it merely amounted
to my being made Stroke-oar of the third
row of the Dey's State-barge, or Galleasse.
Imagine me now, in a Tunic and Drawers
of Scarlet Serge, and a White Turban round

my Head to keep me from Sun-stroke, chained by the Ankles to a bench, and with an Iron Collar round my Neck, from which another Chain passed to a Bar running fore and aft the whole length of the Galleasse. Between the benches of Rowers runs a narrow Planking; and up and down this continually patrols a great Tawny Ruffian of a Moorish Boatswain, armed with a Whip of Rhinoceros Hide, which, with a Will, he lays on to the Shoulders of those who do not tug hard enough at the Oar. Miserable and fallen as was my state, I did yet manage to evade the crowning Degradation of Stripes; for, being a Man used to the Sea, and full of Courageous Activity, I got through my toil so as to make it impossible for my Superiors to find fault with me; and besides, in a few words of Lingua Franca that I picked up, I gave the Boatswain to under-stand that if he ever hit me with his Rhi-noceros Thong, I should take the earliest opportunity of Strangling him. As for our Food, 'twas mainly Beans, and in the morn-ing a Mess of boiled Maize they call Cous-

coussou, with some villanous Rank Butter, melted, poured over it.   And sometimes the Carcass of a Sheep that had died of Disease was given to us.   But whatever we had was eaten on our benches, and the Cook of the Galleasse passed up and down the planking to serve out the Rations.   We Ate on our benches, we Slept on our benches, and some of us died on our benches.   There were Ninety-two Christian Slaves on board the Dey's Galleasse, and Twelve on my Bench. Being Stroke-oar, I was spared the continual contemplation of a Man's back in front of me, which other Slaves have told me makes you so mad that you want to Bite him ; but 'twas scarcely less Vexatious to have behind, as I had, a Chattering Fellow of a French-man, for ever jabbering forth his complaints, and not bearing them with the surly Dignity of a Briton.   I could almost *hear* this fellow grimace ; and he was never tired of bemoaning his bygone happy state as a Hairdresser's Journeyman in the Rue St. Honoré at Paris. "Why did a Vain Ambition prompt me to journey from Marseilles to Constantinople?"

cried he about Fifty times a day. "Why did I rely on the protection of my Wife's Cousin, who gave me recommendations to his brother, Cook-in-Chief to the Ambassador of France at the court of the Antique Byzantium (*l'antique Byzance*)? Where is my Wife? Where is my Wife's Cousin? They are drinking the wine of Ramponneau ; they are dancing at the Barriers. Oh, my Cocotte! where is my Cocotte?"

" Hang your Cocotte !" I used to cry out in a rage. " 'Tis bad enough to be mewed up here like a Bear in a pit, without being worried by a counfounded Barber's Clerk !"

I had been Tugging at the Oar full Six Months, when a change came over my lamentable Lot. The Dey of Algiers was at this time one Mahomet Bassa, a very Bold, Fierce, Fighting Man, but of the meanest Extraction, and one, indeed, that had been no more than a common Soldier, from which he had sprung to be, by turns, Oda-Bashee or Lieutenant, Bullock-Bashee or Captain, Tiah-Bashee or Colonel, and Aga or General. For among these strange

people every valiant and aspiring Soldier,—
I wish 'twas so in England,—though taken
yesterday from the Plough, may be considered as Heir-Apparent to the Throne.
Nor are. they ashamed of the obscurity of
their birth.　This Mahomet Bassa, in a dispute he once had with the Spanish Consul,
said : "My mother sold Sheep's Trotters,
and my father Neat's Tongues; but they
would have been ashamed to expose for sale
on their stalls a Tongue so worthless as
thine."　Mahomet Bassa was, like most of
the Turks, a man of Pleasure, and his Harem
was furnished with an extraordinary number
of choice Beauties.

His Highness (as he is called), happening
to single me out from the rest of the Slaves
on board of the Galleasse, and being told that
I was English—for equally in hopes of
Bettering my Condition, and for the purpose
of keeping Secret my Employment with his
Eminence, I had avowed myself to be of
that Nation—ordered me to be released
from my Chains, and brought before him at
the Divan.　Through his Interpreter, a

cunning Rogue from Corfu, who spoke most Languages indifferently well, he asked me who I was, and how I came to be aboard the Speronare. I answered, conveniently mixing fact with fiction, that I had been a Captain by Sea and Land in the Service of the King of England; that I had earned a good deal of Prize-Money; had retired from Active Duties, being now nigh upon Fifty years of Age, and was taking my pleasure by voyaging in a part of Europe with which I had hitherto been little acquainted. This Answer seemed to satisfy him pretty well; although he was very curious to know whether I had any Kindred in the Island of Malta, or any foregathering among the Knights. Fortunately for me the Interpreter, to whom I had given a hint of ultimate Reward, deposed that I could not speak twenty words of Maltese (which is a kind of Bastard Italian); and he told me that if it had been discovered that I was in any way Connected with the Order, I should surely have been Impaled; the Dey being then in a towering rage with the Knights, one of whose commanders had just captured one of his finest Brigantines, and Dressed Ship, as he humorously put it, by hanging every Man-Jack of the Crew at the Yard-arm, and the Algerine Captain at the Mizen. The Dey then asked me if I had any Friends who I thought would pay my Ransom, the which he placed at the Moderate Computation of Four Thousand Gold Achmedies (about Fifteen Hundred Pounds sterling). I answered, that I thought I could raise about half that Sum, if I were allowed to communicate with one Monsieur Foscue, a Banker at Marseilles, upon whom I had—or rather my Captors had—a Letter of Credit, which they had taken from me. But by Ill-luck this Letter of Credit could not be found. The Captain and Crew of the Rover that took the Speronare were all well bastinadoed about it, but no Letter was forthcoming; and I am more inclined to think that it was thrown, in sheer Ignorance, overboard, than that it was Embezzled. However, as 'twas not to be discovered, they Dey began to look upon me as an Impostor; but I earnestly represented to the Interpreter that, if I had time to write to Monsieur Foscue, all would be right. This I had his Highness's gracious permission to do, and meanwhile was to remain a Slave; but was not sent back to the Galleys. Being a Strong Fellow, and professing to know something about Gardening—Lord help me! I had never touched a Spade ten times in my Life—I was sent to work in his Highness's Gardens at the Castle of Sitteet-ako-Leet. As for my Letter, I penned it in as good French as I could muster, begging Monsieur Foscue to communicate at once with his Eminence, telling him how I had been captured, and that my Letter of Credit had been taken from me, and of the Sorry Plight I was now in. I was given to understand that from Six to Nine Months must pass by before I could expect an Answer; for that Safe Conducts to Christian Packets between Algiers and Marseilles were only granted thrice a

year, and the last was but just departed.
Whereupon I resigned myself to my Captivity, hoping for Better Days.

The Head Gardener of the Dey was an
old Renegado German, named Baupwitz,
who tried hard to convert me to the Mussulman Faith.   But in addition to my stanch
Attachment to the Protestant Religion, I
could see that the State and Condition of
the few Renegados in Algiers was very
mean and miserable, and that they were
despised alike by Turks, Moors, Arabs,
Bedoweens, and Jews.   And, indeed, what
good had Baupwitz done himself by turning
Paynim ?   Thus much I put to him plainly;
at which the Old Man was angered, and for
some days used me very spitefully ; when
the Dey, coming to the Castle, took it into
his head to have me brought back to
Algiers, and enrolled among his Musicians
as a Player upon the Cymbals.   I declare
that although able to troll out a Stave now
and then, I could not so much as Whistle
" God save the King ;" but I managed to
clash my two Saucepan-Lids or Cymbals

together and to make a Noise, which is all the Turks care for, they having no proper Ear for Music. As one of his Highness's Musicians, I was dressed very grandly, with a monstrous Turban all covered with Gold Spangles and Silk Tassels ; but I had a Collar of Silver riveted round my Neck, and Silver Shackles round my Ancles, and Silver Manacles round my Wrists ; and was still a Slave.

The rest of the Musicians were either Black Negroes or Cophtic Christians, and they used me with Decent Civility ; nor did the Master of the Musicians—otherwise a most cruel Moor—go out of his way to flout, much less smite me with his Rattan. If he had dared but to lay one Stripe upon me, I would have sprang upon the Wretch and dashed out his Brains with my Cymbals, even if I had been put upon the Pale for it half an hour afterwards.

Lodged in the Guard-house at the Dey's Palace, with pretty abundant Rations, and some few Piastres daily to buy Wine (I being a Frank) and Tobacco, and pretty well

treated by the Cologlies, or Moorish Soldiers, I did not pass such a very bad time of
it; and when off Duty, had liberty to go
about the City and Suburbs pretty much as
I chose.   And I was a hundred times better
off than the Moslem Slaves are at Malta.

These Algerines are an Uncouth, Savage
People; and the Turkish Despotism has
quite destroyed that security and Liberty
which of old gave birth and encouragement
to Learning: hence the knowledge of Medicine, Philosophy, and the Mathematics,
which once so flourished among the Arabs,
is now almost entirely lost.   The Children
of the Moors and Turks are sent to School
at about Six years old, where they are
taught to Read and Write for the value of
about a Penny a week of our Money.
Instead of Paper or a Slate, each boy has a
piece of thin square Board, slightly daubed
over with Whiting; on this he makes his
Letters, which may be wiped off or renewed
at pleasure.   Having made some progress
in the Koran, he is initiated into the Cere-
monies and Mysteries of the Mahometan

Religion; and when he has distinguished himself in any of these branches of Learning, he is Richly Dressed, mounted on a Horse finely Caparisoned, and paraded, amidst the Huzzas of his School-fellows, through the Streets; while his Friends and Relations assemble to congratulate his Parents, and load him with Toys and Sweetmeats. And this Observance answers to our Western Rite of Confirmation. But after being three or four years at School, the Boys are put 'Prentice to Trades or enrolled in the Army, where they very speedily forget all they have learnt.

Though such bold Sailors, the Algerines are very despicable as Navigators. Their chief Astronomer, Muley Hamet Ben Daoud, when I was there, who superintended and regulated the Hours of Prayer by the Moon and Stars, had not the skill to make a Sun-dial; and in Navigation they cannot get beyond Pricking of a Chart, and distinguishing the Eight principal Points of the Compass. Even Chemistry, which was once the favourite Science of these people, is

at present only applied to the Distilling of
a little Rose-water. The Physicians chiefly
study the Spanish Translation of Dioscorides
(that was a Learned Leech in Olden Times);
but the Figures of the Plants and Animals
are more consulted than the Descriptions:
yet are these Knaves naturally Subtle and
Ingenious; wanting nothing but Applica-
tion and Patronage to cultivate and improve
their Faculties. They are for the most part
Predestinarians, and pay little regard to
Physic, either leaving the Disorder to con-
tend with Nature, or making use of Charms
and Incantations. They, however, resort
to the Hammam, or Hot Bagnio (a great
Sweating-bath, and a sovereign Remedy for
most Distempers), and have a few Specifics
in general use. Thus, in Pleurisy and the
Rheumatics they make several Punctures on
the part affected with a Red-hot Needle;
and into simple Gun-shot Wounds they
pour Fresh Butter almost boiling hot. The
Prickly Pear roasted in Ashes is applied to
Bruises, Swellings, and Inflammations; and
a dram or two of the Round Birthwort is

esteemed the best remedy in the world for the Choler. But few Compound Medicines; only, for that dreadful scourge the Plague (from which Lord deliver all Men not being Heathens!), they commonly use a Mixture of Myrrh, Saffron, Aloes, and Syrup of Myrtle-berries,—which does not hinder 'em from dying like Sheep with the Rot.

There are no Public Clocks here; those contrivances, with Bells, being held an Impious Aping of Providence. And the only way you have of telling the Time is by the Fellows up in the Minarets calling 'em to Prayers. Some of the rich Agas have Watches, bought or stolen out of Europe; but they are usually spoilt by the Women of the Harem playing with 'em. The Dey's principal Wife, Zoraïde Khanum, is said to have boiled a large Gold Chronometer, made by Silvain of Paris, with Cream and Sweet Almonds. Yet does a remnant of their Ancestors' old skill in Arithmetic and Algebra linger among 'em; for whereas not One in Twenty Thousand can do an Equation (and Captain Blokes taught me, and I have since forgotten How), yet the Merchants are frequently very dexterous in Reckoning by Memory, and have also a singular method of Numeration, by putting their hands into each other's Sleeves, and touching one another with this or that Finger, or a particular joint, each standing for a determined Sum or Number.   Thus, without ere moving their lips,—and your Mussulman has a wholesome horror of squandering Words,—they conclude Bargains of the Greatest Value.

None of the Women think themselves completely Adorned till they have tinged the Lashes and the edges of their Eyelids with the powder of Lead-Ore. This they do by dipping a Bodkin of the thickness of a Quill into the Powder, and dragging it under the Eyelids. This gives their Eyes a Sooty colour, but is thought to add a Wonderful Grace to their Complexions. And was not this that which Jezebel did in the Ancient Time?* The Old Custom of plighting their Troth by drinking out of each

* 2 Kings, ix. 30.

other's Hand is the only Ceremony used by
the Algerines at their Marriages. The
Bridegroom may put away his Wife when-
ever he pleases, upon the forfeiture of the
Dowry he has settled upon her; but he
cannot afterwards take her again until she
has been Re-married and Divorced from
another Man. After all, the Wives are
only held as a better class of Servants, that
when their Toil is over become Toys. The
greater part of the Moorish Women would
be esteemed Beauties even in England, and
as Children they have the finest Complexions
in the World; but at Thirty they become
Wrinkled Old Women. For a Girl is often
a Mother at Eleven, and a Grandmother at
Twenty-two; and their Lives being generally
as long as Europeans, these Matrons often
live to see Children of many Generations.
They are desperately Superstitious, and
hang the Figure of an Open Hand round
the Necks of their Children; and never an
Algerine Pirate goes out of Port without
such a Hand painted on the Stern, as a
counter Charm to an Evil Eye. Truly there

are some Christian Folks not much less foolish in their Superstitions ; and Rich and Poor among the Neapolitans carry a forked bit of Coral about with them, to conjure away this same Evil Eye, which they call *Gettatura.*

They have a kind of Monks called Marabutts, who are supposed to lead an Austere Life, and pass their lives in counting a Chaplet of Ninety-nine Beads ; but who are, in truth, Impudent Beggars, Thieves, and Profligates. And this is pretty well the Character of the whole body of Algerines, from the Dey in his Palace to his Father who sells Sheep's Trotters. There are a few Grave People, in no constant Employ (that it is to say, they have made their fortunes by Murder and Piracy, and are now Retired), who spend the day, either in conversing with one another at the Barber's Shops, or at the Bazaars and Coffee-houses. But the greater part of the Moorish and Turkish Youth are the wildest of Gallants and Roysterers, and waste their time in the most unseemly Fandangoes.

Item.—These Marabutts are no better than the Mountebanks I have seen at the Carnival of Venice or at Southwark Fair. One Seedy Mustapha tells me that a neighbouring Marabutt had a solid Iron Bar, which, upon command, would give the same Report and do as much Mischief as a Piece of Cannon. At Seteef, too, there was one famous for Vomiting Fire; but the Renegado Baupwitz, who had seen him, assured me 'twas all a trick; that his Mouth did certainly seem to be all in a Blaze, while he counterfeited Violent Agony; but that on close inspection it appeared that the Flames and Smoke with which he was surrounded arose from Tow and Sulphur, which he had contrived to kindle under his Hyke. The most commendable thing I can find in the Algerine Character is the great respect they pay to their Dead. They don't cram 'em into stifling little Graveyards in the midst of crowded towns, as we do, to our injury and shame; but have large Burial-grounds, at a good distance from their towns and villages. Each Family has a particular

Part, walled in like a garden, where the Bones of their Ancestors have remained undisturbed for many generations. The Graves are all distinct and separate, and the space between as planted with Beautiful Flowers, bordered round with Stone, or paved over with Tiles. The Graves of the Great People are likewise distinguished by Square Rooms with Cupolas built over them, which, being kept constantly clean, whitewashed, and beautified, nevertheless continue like the hypocrites, and are but Sepulchres full within of nothing but Dead Men's Bones.

It happened one fine Autumnal Afternoon, that, my Services as Cymbal-Player not being required until the Dey's Supper after Evening Prayers, I was wandering for mere Amusement in some of the least-frequented Streets of the City; which are here, for the sake of Shade, mere narrow Lanes, without any Pavement but Dust, and without a Door or Window from twenty yards to twenty yards. In fact they are but Passages between almost dead walls;

the Houses themselves generally standing in the midst of the Gardens. Now I quitted the Street of Baba-zoun by the Street of the Shroffs, or Money-changers, designing to reach the Gate of the River; but the Streets are all so much alike that I lost my Way, and went blundering on from one Lane into another, till I almost despaired of finding my Road back again. I should be too late for the Dey's Supper, thought I; and although Jack Dangerous was never given to Trembling, I began to feel very uncomfortable concerning the Notice that Mahomet Bassa, who was never known to have Pity on any Human Being, Man, Woman, or Child, might take of my Absence. For these accursed Algerines are most cruel in their Punishments. Trials are very swift, and Sentence is always executed within half an hour afterwards. Small Offences are punished with the Bastinado, or the Rhinoceros Whip. For Clipping or Debasing the Public Coin the old Egyptian punishment of cutting off the Hands is inflicted, although the Dey, in one of his Furies, has been known to have the Base Money melted and poured down the Coiner's Throat.   If a Jew or a Christian is guilty of Murder, he is Burnt alive without the gates of the City ; but for the same Crime the Moors and Arabs are either Impaled, hung up by the Neck over the Battlements of the City, or thrown upon Hooks fixed upon the Walls, below, where they sometimes hang in Dreadful Torments for Thirty and Forty hours together before they Expire. The Turks, however, out of respect for their Characters, are sent to the Aga's house, where they are either Bastinadoed or Strangled ; and when the Women offend, they are not exposed to the populace, but are sent to a private House of Correction ; or, if the Crime be Capital, they are sewn up in a Sack, carried out to Sea, and Drowned. And for especial Criminals is reserved the Extraordinary Barbarous punishment of Sawing Asunder ; for which purpose they prepare two Boards, of the same length and breadth as the Unfortunate Person, and,

having tied him betwixt them, begin sawing
at the Head, and so proceed till he is divided
into Halves. 'Tis said that Kardinash, a
person who was not long since Ambassador
at the Court of England, suffered in this
wise merely for maintaining, in the face of
the Dey, that the King of Great Britain
had only One Wife.

All these Grim Probabilities did I revolve
in my mind, as the Sun went on sinking,
and I could meet nothing but a few Rap-
scallion Boys that, when I strove to stammer
out a few words of Arabic to ask my Way,
laughed and jeered in their Impudent manner,
and flung handfuls of Dust at me.   Just as
I was losing all Patience, and determined to
Knock at the first door I came to, and make
my state known at all hazards, there came
upon me at the corner of a street the Figure
of a Woman, Muffled up, as 'tis their fashion,
in her Hyke and Burnouse, so that I could
only see her Eyes, which were smeared over
with the usual Black Stuff, but which seemed
to have somewhat of a Yellowish Cast.   I
started, as if she were a Ghost just risen

from the ground; but indeed she had only just stepped out from a little Garden-door, that now stood Ajar. From the folds of her White Burnouse now came out a plump Hand, very Glossy, but very Black. She first laid her Finger on that part of her Hyke where her Mouth might be, to command me to silence; then touched me on the Arm; then pointed to a Latticed Window high up in the wall, to give me to understand that some one had been Watching me from there; and then beckoned me to Follow her. I was wofully perplexed, and, thought I, "The Dey will have no Cymbals to his Supper to-night, that's certain." Still, it is never to be said that J. D. ever shirked an adventure that promised aught of Love or Peril; and had it been into the jaws of a Lion, I must have followed the Negro Emissary. After all, I reasoned, I was a proper-looking Fellow, although no longer in my First Youth, and my hair beginning to whiten somewhat; but Love levels ranks, as my Lord Grizzle has it in Tom Thumb; and I was, perhaps, not the first Frank Slave who was favoured by a beauteous Moorish Lady. A Moorish Beauty! Why, this might be, after all, a Princess, a Sultana, a Turkish Khanum! It turned out, however, far differently from what I had expected. Following the Slave, we quitted the street and passed through a Porch, or Gateway, which the Negress carefully locked after her. We now entered upon a Court, with Benches on either side, and paved very handsomely with Marble, covered in the middle with a rich Turkey Mat, and sheltered from the heat of the weather by a kind of Veil, expanded by Ropes from one side of the Parapet-wall, or Lattice of the Flat Roof, to the other. So into a little Cloister running round this Court, and up a little winding stone Staircase into another Cloister or Upper Gallery. Then at a Door all covered with rich Filigree-work in Gold and Colours did the Negress knock; and by and by a soft silvery Voice, of which the sound, somehow, made me start and tremble much more than that of the Old Knight of Malta had done, said a few words in Arabic, and we went in.

I found myself in a large square Apartment, with curious latticed Windows, through which the Evening Sunlight came, in the prettiest of patterns, and fell, like so many spangles disposed by an artful Embroiderer, upon the rich Carpet. A great Divan, or stuffed Bench of Crimson Damask, ran all round the room, with many soft pillows and shawls upon it; and on this Divan, upon the side opposite the door, sat an Eastern Lady, amazingly Dressed. She had laid aside her Hyke, which was of white silk gorgeously striped with gold and crimson Bars, and all dotted with Bullion Tassels, and sat in a tight-fitting jacket of Red Velvet, open in front, where you could see the Bosom of her Snowy Smock all blazing with Emeralds and Rubies. I had never seen so many of the latter kind of Jewels since the days of my Grandmother, in her Cabinet of Relics. Round her Waist was swathed a great Cashmerian Shawl, very rich and noble, and with a heavy Fringe; and from among the folds peeped out a little Poniard with a jewelled Hilt, and a knife with a Gold and Mother-of-pearl Haft to cut her Victuals. She wore loose Trowsers, or Drawers, of a very fine spun silk, covered with a raised pattern in gold thread, that, as is the custom of the Moorish Women, were fastened at the Knee, and then fell in quite a torrent of Drapery down to her Ankles, nearly covering her pretty Feet. A sweet Fashion, and very Modest. As to the Feet themselves,—the smallest, sure, that mortal woman ever had,—I could, rapid as was my survey, see that she wore no Hose; but her tiny Toes were thrust into Slippers or Papowshes of blue velvet, all heightened and enriched with Gold Orris and Seed Pearls. On her head was a dainty little cap, of the Fez Pattern, but of velvet instead of cloth, jewelled; and from it hung a monstrous Tassel of Gold, which reached half-way down the Back. As for her Hair, it hung very nearly down to the ground, being all collected into one Lock, and bound and plaited with Ribbons; and being thus adorned, were tied close together above the Lock, the several corners of a Kerchief, made of thin flexible plates of Gold, cut through, and engraved in imitation of Lace. In one hand she held a great Fan, of Peacock's Feathers, with a Mirror in the midst, and a handle of Gold, Emeralds, and Agate, that would have driven a Duke's-Place Jew crazy to look at; and in the other,—well, you know that Oriental Fashions are different from ours, and that the Paynim nations have the strangest of Manners and Customs,—I declare that in the other Hand—the dexter one—the Lady held the Tube of a Tobacco-pipe, the which she was smoking with great Deliberation and apparent Relish. But 'twas a very different Pipe to what we are in the habit of seeing in England—having a Bowl of fine Red Clay encrusted with Gems, a long straight tube of Cherry-wood, and a Mouth-piece of Amber studded with Precious Stones. This Pipe they call a Chibook, and they smoke it much as we do our common Clay things; but there's another, which they call a Nargilly, like the Hubble-bubble smoked by the proud Planters in the Dutch East Indies. With the Nargilly, the Smoke passes first through Rose-water, to purify it; and after passing through many snake-like coils of silk and wire tubing, the Smoker gulps it down bodily; so that it goes into his Lungs, and must make them as sooty as a foul Chimney. Many of the Turks are so handy at this nasty trick, that they can make the Smoke they have swallowed come out of their ears, eyes, and nostrils; but I envy them not such Mountebankery, and when I smoke my Pipe, am content to Blow a Cloud in a moderate and Christian manner.

I have kept you so long describing this Eastern Lady's Dress, that you must be growing impatient to know whether her Face matched in handsomeness with her Apparel; but there was the Deuce of it; for while I stood before her, staring and wondering over her splendid Habiliments, I could catch ne'er a glimpse of her Countenance, which was entirely concealed from view by the Veil they call a *Formah*, which is made of a very fine gauzy stuff, but painted in body-colour in a pattern so as to make it Opaque, and so artfully disposed as to hide the Face without shading any of the splendour of the Dress. And though I could not make out so much as the tip of the Lady's Nose, I had a queer sensation that she was looking at *me*, nay, even that her eyes were twinkling in a merry manner under her Veil. And so I remained Dumbfoundered, quite uncertain as to the kind of Adventure that had befallen me. Had some Moorish or Turkish Dame designed only to Divert herself at the expense of a poor Christian Slave? or was the Veiled Lady only some artful Adventuress of the Jewish, Armenian, or Cophtic Nation, of whom there were many here, affecting great magnificence in their Habits and Living?

Full Ten Minutes had the Lady so gazed upon me, I staring stupidly at her, and the Negress continuing to enjoin me to silence by putting her finger to her Lips. Then clapping her little hands together (I mean that the Lady did, for the Black Woman's were sad Paws), in tumbles from a little door at the side of the Divan a Negro Urchin about eight years of age, very richly clad, who at her command brings Pipes and Coffee; and, signs being made to me, I sat down on a couple of Pillows on the Ground, smoked a Chibook, emptied a Cup, not much bigger than an egg-shell, of Coffee,— very Bitter and Nauseous here, for they give you the Dregs as well as the Liquor,— all the while staring at the Lady as though my Eyeballs would have started out of my Head. And by this time the Sun had quite gone down, and as there is but little Twilight in these parts, the Shade of Evening fell like a great black Pall over the Room; so the little Black Urchin came tumbling in again with a couple of Lamps, which he set down before the Divan. These cast a very soft and rosy Light, passing through folds of Pink Silk; and as soon as my eyes grew accustomed to 'em, I could see that the Lady had raised her Veil, that she was looking upon me with a pair of Dark, Roguish, Twinkling Orbs, and that I was sitting in the presence of my kind Protectress, Lilias.

"What think you of this for an Opera Habit, goodman Cerberus?" cried she. "Is this not much better than the Ballet of Orpheus? And, goodness! what strange Accoutrement have you, too, got into?"

When my first ecstasies of Joy and Amazement were over, I explained to my Dear Patroness the Reasons (none of my own choosing) for appearing in such a Garb as I then wore; telling her how I had been Galley-Slave, and was now Cymbal Player, to the Unbelieving Dey of Algiers; and with great Humility did I ask after her Honoured Parent, and seek to know by what uncommon Accident she, the erst Ballet Dancer in the King's Opera-House at Paris, had come to be the tenant of this Outlandish House, and arrayed in this Heathen Habit. She answered me with that Candour and Simplicity which I ever found characteristic of her. Old Mr. Lovell was still alive, and in Paris; and this is how his Daughter had become separated from him. A very brilliant Engagement, as First Dancer, indeed, had been offered to her at the King's Theatre at Palermo; and, after long unsuccessful importunities addressed to the Gentlemen of the French King's Chamber to cancel her Engagement, these instances, owing to the untiring influence of Cardinal de ———, had succeeded, and she was allowed to depart. Full willingly would she have taken her Papa with her as a Travelling Companion; but the Old Gentleman was now very Infirm, and averse from Moving; and so Lilias was placed under the Guardianship of an old Spanish Lady, the Señora Satisfacion de Mismar, who was the Palermo Manager's Aunt, made his engagements for him abroad, and played the Duenna or Singing Old Woman in his Comedies and Operas at home. Nothing could be properer than this arrangement, Donna Satisfacion being a Personage of exceeding Discretion and Propriety of Behaviour; so the two, with half a dozen more little Dancing-girls that had been hired to fill inferior places, started for Bordeaux, whence they designed to take shipping for Palermo. But by ill luck there was no Packet or Merchant Vessel bound for Sicily to be taken up for a long time; and so they were fain to travel to Toulon, avoiding Marseilles, where the Plague then was very bad, and thence by way of Nizza to Genoa, where they found a Brig bound for Messina, which they thought would serve their turn. And, in truth, the poor souls found it but too well served; for the Brig was captured off Bastia in Corsica by one of these diabolical Barbary Rovers, all on board made Slaves, and carried, not into Algiers, but into Sallee. There, after much suffering, poor Donna Satisfacion de Mismar died of a Distemper of the country, and poor Lilias was left without any other Protector than her own Virtue and a kind Providence.

'Twas a terrible condition to be left in: Young, Fair, Friendless, and a Slave among these Moorish Barbarians. By Heaven's Mercy, however, the dear Girl came to no

Harm. 'Tis the custom, before the Christian Women-captives are exposed for sale in the public Slave-Market, where they are Handled and put through their paces as though they were so many Cattle, for a Private Inspection of 'em to be made by the rich Persons of the place, who come and take Pipes and Coffee with the Merchant, glance over his Stock in a respectful Manner, and often strike a Bargain there and then. The Girls for sale are apparelled in a sumptuous manner, bathed, perfumed, and trinketed out for their Private View; and their Captors seek to render 'em docile by giving 'em plenty of Sweetmeats. As if the intolerable pangs of Slavery were to be allayed by Lollipops! It chanced that among the visitors to the Merchant's House was one Hamet Abdoollah, a very Learned Man, a Physician by Trade, and equally trusted by the Bey of Tunis, the Dey of Algiers, and him who reigned at Tripoli; but who would not devote himself to the service of any of these Potentates, but, loving an independent life, served all with equal fidelity, sometimes

even travelling so far as the Capital of
Morocco, where he was in high favour with
the Savage who calls himself Emperor of
that country, which would be as piratical as
the Barbary States, only it has less Sea-
board. The father of this Physician had
been quite as learned a Man as he, and by
the name of Muley Abdoollah had travelled
much in Western Europe, where by his
Skill and Erudition he had gained so much
consideration among the Polite as to be
elected a Correspondent Member of the
Royal Society of England and the Paris
Academy of Sciences. His son was one of
the wisest and justest and most merciful of
his Species, as you will presently have cause
to admit. He was struck at once by the
Beauty, Intelligence, and Goodness of Lilias,
and his humane heart recoiled at the thought
of what her fate might have been among a
people given up to Cruelty and Lust. He
forthwith bought her of the Merchant at a
fair price ; for although that crafty and rapa-
cious Slave-Dealer would have made him pay
Through the Nose for his Treasure, knowing

the Physician to be a man of great Wealth, he forbore in very shame from his extortion; for Hamet Abdoollah had but just saved his little son out of a Fever, after he had been given up by all the Ignorant Leeches of Sallee.

So Lilias became the Bond-servant, but only so in name, to this Wise and Good Man. As her dearest wish was now to rejoin her Father, he undertook to send her back to France, and with that view did remove with his precious charge to Algiers, only exacting from her a promise that while she remained under his protection she would wear the Moorish Habit and pass as his Wife, so as to avoid Insult when she walked abroad. -But of any thoughts of Love and Intrigue the Good Man was entirely free. He was wrapped up in the study of the Healing Art, and troubled his head much more about Drugs, Cataplasms, and Electuaries, than about the Bow and Arrows of Dan Cupid. Though why the God of Love should have been christened Daniel, it puzzles me to comprehend. This accounts for the manner in which I had found my dear Protectress caparisoned in every respect as a Moorish Dame. She told me that this was by no means the first time she had seen me, and that my being Cymbal-Player in the Dey's Musicians was very well known to her, and that her kind Guardian was on the point of petitioning the Dey to release me from Servitude, when by accident she espied me from the Window, and could not resist the temptation of having me called in.

But, in her sweet regard for what was due to Modesty and Decorum, she would have no Parley with me save in the presence of the Black slave,—'tis true that she did not understand a word of English—and directly she had come to an end of her Narrative, she sent the Tumbling Urchin to inquire whether the Physician had come home, the part of the House she occupied being quite separate and distinct from his. The smutty little Imp comes back bringing word that Hamet would wait upon her presently ; and anon, after discreetly tapping at the door, he came in, a grave, Reverend Man, in a

flowing Robe of Sad-coloured Taffety, and
with a long White Beard and Green Turban ;
for he had made the Mecca Pilgrimage, and
yet abstained from assuming the title of
Hadji, to which he was entitled. He spoke
very good French, and even a little English
(learned from his Papa); and when I was
made known to him, asked for news of Dr.
Mead and Sir Hans Sloane, although I could
tell him but little of that worthy and
deceased Gentleman.

" Happy is the Wooing that is not long
a Doing," they say ; and, by this time, you
will probably have discovered that I Loved
Lilias Lovell very dearly. 'Twas no Ramp-
ing, Rantipoling, Fiery-Furnace kind of
Calf Love on my part, but a matured anp
sensible admixture of Gratitude and Sincere
Affection. I scorn to conceal that although
I knew myself to be by Lineage worthy the
hand of a Gentleman's Daughter,* I was

---

* I preserve a fragment of what His Eminence
was pleased once upon a time to write to me, in his
curious Italian way of spelling the French tongue :

aware that, by the Meanness of the condition under which I was first known to the Lovell Family, a Gulf yawned between their Estate and mine; and that, warm and devoted as was my Love for the Pretty Little Creature I had saved from the Flames, I could but deem that she reckoned the Humane Dog Cerberus of the Opera Ballet as of no greater account than a real Doggish Mastiff. But, to my extreme Amazement and Felicity, this was not so. I was beloved by this amiable Young Person, to whom Ambassadors were proud to go on their knees, and whom Gentlemen of the Chamber would have covered with Diamonds. With a charming frankness, blushing and stammering, yet with Virginal Pride, she confessed that she was enamoured of me, and, if Fortune were propitious, would gladly be my Wife. I could at first scarcely realize the possibility of such great

-----

" *Si cieu che vous m'avez dict sur vostre Naissance à vray, vos esteo digne di monter dedans le carozze du Roy.*"

and unmerited Happiness; for well did I know the disparity in Age that existed between us — how Rough and Weather-beaten was I; and she, how Tender, Delicate, and Good! "But does not the Ivy twine round the Oak?" quoth the Physician, as he smote me cheerfully on the Shoulder. And behold, now, gnarled and battered old Jack Dangerous, with this delicious little Parasite creeping toward and Nestling Round him.

CHAPTER THE NINTH AND LAST.

OF MY SERVICE UNDER THE GREAT TURK AS A BASHAW ·
    OF MY ADVENTURES IN RUSSIA AND OT
    TRIES ; AND OF MY COMING HOME AT LAS⸱ —
    BUYING MY GRANDMOTHER'S HOUSE (WHICH IS NOW
    MINE) IN HANOVER SQUARE.

'TWAS the advice of the Good Physician, that, to prevent Accidents, we should be Married without delay; for in these hot countries you are here to-day and gone to-morrow, and no one can tell what may happen. Difficulties almost insurmountable, 'tis true, seemed to stand in the way of our Union; but Hamet Abdoollah was able to act almost a Magician's part to bring about our Happiness. I was for the time being bestowed in his House, and the next morning the Physician hies him to the Dey, who was in a Fury about me, and was threatening all kinds of Bowstrings and Bastinadoes. But his Highness happening likewise to be suffering from Toothache, and as a Man with a Raging Tooth would give all the Treasures of Potosi to be quit of his Agony, the Physician promised to Relieve him forthwith if he would grant his Suit. The Dey promised him any thing he could wish for, and so Hamet Abdoollah cures him with a little Phial full of nothing but Tar Balsam. 'Tis but just to the Mussulmans to say, that when they have once given their Word of Honour, they keep it with Extreme Rigour; so that when the Physician begged pardon for me, and License to purchase me out of the Dey's service and take me into his own, the Suit was very cheerfully granted. Joyfully Hamet Abdoollah repairs to us again, with a Firman under the Dey's own Signet granting me my Liberty; and that very forenoon my silver Collar, Anklets, and Manacles were stricken off,—the Physician returning them to the Dey's Treasury,—and I was no longer a Slave.

Although there is no Man alive who mislikes Popery and its Superstitious Practices more than does J. D., there is one order of Nuns and one of Monks for whose members I entertain a profound Love and Reverence. Of She-Religious, I mean those Blessed Sisters of Charity who go about the World doing good, braving Sickness, succouring Misery, assuaging Hunger, drying up Tears, and smiling in the Face of Death: God bless those Holy Women, say I, wheresoever they are to be found! and in our own Protestant country of England, why should we not have similar Sisterhoods of Women of Mercy, or Deaconesses, bound by no rigid vows, and suffering no ridiculous Penances of Stripes and Macerations, but obeying only the call of Religious Charity, and going Quietly and Trustfully about their Master's Business ?   Of He-Monks, I mean the Fathers of the Work of Redemption, or Redemptorists, whose sole business it is to travel about Begging and Praying of the Rich for money to Ransom poor Christian bodies out of Slavery; which is a better

work, I think, than praying for the deliverance of their Souls out of Purgatory.
These Redemptorist Fathers have a per-
manent Station and Correspondence at all
the Piratical Ports of the Barbary Coast;
and at stated times, when they have gathered
enough Money to redeem a certain number
of Christians, a body of the Fraternity visit
the Station, take away their Sanctified Merchandise, and by their Humble and Devout
Carriage, and exemplary Poverty of Life,
extort admiration even from the Bloodthirsty Heathens.

Now at Algiers, about this time, there
was suffered to dwell an old Religious of
this Order, Le Père Lefanu,—who for his
Virtues and Piety was esteemed even by the
Mussulman Ulemas, and was thought a good
deal more of than any of their Marabutts
or Santons, which is a name they give to a
kind of wandering Idiots, who, the Crazier
they are, are thought the more deserving of
Superstitious Veneration. Père Lefanu was
nearly ninety years of age, and had dwelt
among these Barbarians for full sixty years.

of his Life, passing his time in Meditation,
Prayer, and the Visitation of the Sick and
Needy, both among the Unbelievers and the
Christian Slaves, and at the same time trans-
acting all necessary business with the Dey's
Head-men for periodically redeeming those
that were in Bondage. Our good Physician
had a profound esteem for this Reverend
Person, and often visited him; and now it
was through his Ministry that Lilias and I
were to be made One. I had forgotten to
say, that my departed Saint was of the Communion opposite to mine; but in a land of
Pagans 'tis as well to forget all differences
between Papists and Protestants, and to remember only that we are Christians. Père
Lefanu had been ordained a Secular Priest
before he had become a Regular Monk, and
he told me that if I had any Conscientious
Scruples as to the Husband being a Protestant and the Wife of another way of
Thinking, I could have the marriage done
over again in whatever way I thought proper
on our return to Europe. But I was in far
too great a Hurry to be Married to look too

narrowly which way the Cat jumped; and
a Romish Wedding is surely better than
jumping over a Broomstick, which, unless
we had adopted the uncouth Moresque
custom, would have been all the Ceremony
of Matrimony we could have had. So Père
Lefanu came privately, to avoid Gossip, to
the Physician's House, and Lilias Lovell
and John Dangerous were made One in the
French Language, the contracting parties
being English, the Bridegroom's best man
a tawny Mahometan Moor, and the only
Bridesmaid a Black Negress.

Our Honeymoon (we continuing to dwell
in the House of the good Hamet Abdoollah)
was one of unmixed Joy and Gladness; but
'twas too complete to last long, and soon
came a black Storm to lash into fury the
calm surface of our Life's Lake. Seized
with a Malignant Distemper, and after but
three days' Sickness, the good Hamet Abdoollah died. His Pillow was smoothed by
our reverent hands, and with his dying
breath he blessed us. I know not if there
be any Saints in the Mussulman Church;

but if ever a man deserved Canonization from whatsoever Communion he belonged to, I am sure it was Hamet Abdoollah, the Moorish Physician.

His Skill in Medicine had brought him great Wealth, of which, although he was always distributing Alms to the Poor, he left a considerable Portion behind him. In his last moments he sent for the Cadi and Ulema of his Quarter, for his will to be made, or at least to assure them by word of mouth of his Testamentary Intentions, which among this People would have been as religiously carried out as though he had written them. But, alas! when the Cadi and Ulema arrived, he was speechless, and died without word or sign of his Wishes.

His Relations came forthwith to administer to his Effects, and (if truth be not unpalatable to English Heirs, that often do the same thing) to fight and squabble over the administration thereof. A pretty Noise and Riot they made: now weeping and howling over the Corse; now bursting open Trunks, wrenching Trinkets from each other, striving to convey away Garments and Furniture, and even tearing down the hangings of Rich Stuff. Only the Harem, where my one True Wife was, remained inviolate from these Harpies; but me they overwhelmed with the most injurious Invectives and accosted by the foulest epithets, calling me Infidel, Pig, Giaour Dog, Frankish Thief, and the like, telling me that I had fattened long enough on the Substance of a True Believer, with the like opprobrious speeches. I let them have their way, only giving them to understand that the first Man who should attempt to cross the Threshold of my Harem, it were better for him that he never had been Born.

Soon, however, came a greater Heir at Law than any of these, to take possession of the Dead Man's heritage. The news of Hamet Abdoollah's decease had come to the ears of the Dey; and straightway he sends down a strong guard of Coglololies to Seize all in his Name, specially enjoining the Bullock Bashee in command to put the big Christian Slave (meaning myself) in Fetters, and equally secure, although with lighter bonds, the fair Frankish Woman, meaning my dear Wife Lilias. All this was no sooner said than done. The Rough Soldiers burst into the House, and, to prevent any misunderstanding about me, a Cloth (for which I was quite unprepared) was thrown over my head from Behind; and while I was yet struggling to free myself from this blinding Incumbrance, the Gyves were passed over my Wrists and Ankles. And then they removed the Cloth, and, laden with heavy Chains, I had to behold in Despair their Invading the Sanctity of my Harem, and tearing therefrom my Lilias. In vain did I Shout, Threaten, Grind my Teeth, Implore, Promise, and strive to Tear my Hair. They only Laughed; and one Brutish Coglolie made as though to strike me with the flat of his Sabre, when I out with my foot, all fettered as it was, and gave the Ruffian a blow on the Jaw, the which, by the momentum given by the Iron, I thought had stove it in. This much infuriated his Savage Companions; and I doubt not but they

would have finished me, but the Bullock
Bashee, who had orders to the contrary,
constrained them to stay their hand.

What became of my dear Lilias, I was
not allowed to know. She was borne away,
shrieking and calling on me, with Stream-
ing Eyes, for help; and I saw her no more.
Myself they dragged downstairs; and when
we were come into the street, flung me, fettered as I was, over the back of an Artillery
Horse, where I lay, face downwards, and in
a kind of stupor, as listless as a Miller's
Sack; and so, my Gyves jingling and clat-
tering, I was conveyed away.

The cruel and remorseless Dey of Algiers
I saw no more. Some spark of shame there
might perchance be in the Ruffian's Breast
that forbade him to gaze upon the man he
had pardoned and enfranchised, and had
now traitorously Kidnapped. I suppose
that in the Thieves' philosophy of this Fellow he reasoned that, if promises are to be
kept to Live Men, there is no need to keep
them unto Dead ones; that he was released
from all his obligations by the demise of

Hamet Abdoollah; and that, as the Physician could not cure him of the Toothache again, if he chanced to get it, 'twas idle to continue bestowing Favours where no Benefits could be derived.

Into a wretched Dungeon of the Arsenal was poor J. Dangerous thrust, with naught for victuals but Musty Beans and Stinking Water. When I had been here, groaning and gnashing my teeth, for seven days,—which seemed to me thrice seven years,—a Rascally Fellow that I knew to be a Scribe belonging to the Divan of the Dey comes into my Dungeon to tell me that the Packetship has come in from Marseilles, and that in answer to my letter to Monsieur Foscue, that Merchant sends word that he knows nothing at all about me ; to which the Rascally Scribe adds, in the Lingua Franca, that I was no doubt an Impostor who had trumped up a convenient Fable of my being a Gentleman, and having Correspondents who would be Answerable for my Ransom in Europe, in order to get better food and treatment until the real truth could be known. Whereupon he tells me that his Highness the Dey had not yet quite made up his mind as to whether he shall have me Impaled, or merely Flayed Alive, and so slams the door in my Face.

In this Horrible Dungeon did I continue for seven days more, mostly grovelling on the ground, my face downwards, and praying for Deliverance or Death. I had a mind to dash my Brains out against the slimy walls of the Cell, but was only stayed by the thought of my Lilias. 'Twas always night in the abominable Hole, which was lighted only by a hole in the roof, about four inches square, and which gave not into the open air, but into a Corridor above. But on the fifteenth night of my Captivity, for I judged it so by the utter darkness, the door of the Dungeon opened, and the Blessed Old Man that was a Redemptorist Father appeared, bearing a Lantern.

"You have that about you, my son," says he, "which should be a sign that you are a trusted Agent of Holy Mother Church. Can you show it?"

I pointed with one of my fettered hands to my Breast, and made signs for him to search for that he was in quest of. The which he did, and after reverently kissing the Parchment I had between the Glasses, restored it to me.

"You have been most basely entreated," he continued. "Monsieur Foscue sent ample funds for your Ransom, and his Eminence is most anxious for your safety; but the cruel Moorish Prince who governs this unhappy city, after taking the money, feigned that you had made your Escape from the Arsenal, designing to keep you here in Chains and Hunger until you should Perish."

He paused for a moment, for his Great Age made him very feeble, and then continued:

"I can deliver you from this Abode of Misery; but it is not in my power, my son, to give you entire Deliverance. Would that I could! You have but to follow me to the Quayside, where you will find a boat to convey you on board a Turkish Merchant-ship, that to-morrow morning weighs anchor for Constantinople. You will still be a Slave to the Captain, but to your own ingenuity I leave it to obtain complete Freedom.

"And my Wife—my dear, dear Lilias?" I asked.

The Ancient Man shook his head.

"I can do nothing to bring you together again. She cannot follow you to Stamboul; but by Perseverance, and in Time, you may be restored to her."

"Time!" I cried out in bitter desperation. "Time! O Father! I am growing an old man. She is the stay and prop of my Life; she is the one ray of sunshine cast on a Black and Wicked Career! And she is taken from me by these Butchers! and I am to see her no more? What care I for Hunger and Chains, and a Dungeon-floor for a Pallet? They have been familiar to me from my earliest youth. If I am not to have my Lilias's sweet companionship again, I will remain here, in this Hole, and die like a Dog, as I am."

" Take comfort, my son," said the Redemptorist Monk. "Time and Perseverance may, I repeat, enable you to attain your heart's desire. Meanwhile, console yourself with the assurance that the Fair and Good Woman, who is your Wife, is out of peril from lawless men. By the same Packet-ship that brought the Letters from Monsieur Foscue came a Sum sufficient Doubly to Ransom the Young Woman. The benignant protection of his Eminence has been extended to her, and she will in a few days return to France, and to her Father."

" But can I not see her?—cannot I touch her Hand?—can I not press her Lip?—for one brief moment, and for the last time?"

" It is impossible," answered the Monk. " She is watched, both by Day and Night, by zealous agents of the Dey, and I have no means of access to her. 'Twould be death both to you and to myself were I to seek to bring about a meeting between you. Even now the precious moments are wasting away. In another hour the Guard will be changed, and your Escape impossible."

"And how is it possible now?" I asked. "And will no one come to Hurt through my evasion?"

"It *is* possible," he repeated. "You have to walk but from hence to the Outer Gate and the Quayside. Immediately you have departed, the Body of a poor Christian Slave, of your age and stature, who died this morning at the Arsenal, will be conveyed here, and garnished with your Chains. The Dey will be told that you have died in Prison. He loves not to look upon the faces of those he has murdered, and will take the word of the Aga, who is in our pay. Come! there is not an instant to be lost. Here is the key to your Fetters. Unlock them, and follow me."

With a heart that was now elated with the prospect of Deliverance, and now sunk at the thought that I was still to be separated from my Lilias, I did as the good Redemptorist bade me, and, casting my accursed Shackles from me in a heap, limped slowly forth—for the Iron had wofully galled me. Outside the Dungeon-door stood a couple of Coglolies, with their Turban-cloths let down over their faces to serve as Masks, who swiftly unlocked what Doors remained between us and the Sea Rampart. The Monk pressed my Hand, gave me his Blessing, bidding me hope for Better Times, and disappeared. Guided by the Coglolies, and, indeed, half supported by them, I was put into a Boat waiting at the Quayside, as the Monk had told me, and ten minutes' hard pulling brought us alongside a large craft, on board which, I being so weak, they were fain to hoist me with Ropes. By this time I had sunk into a kind of Lethargy, and, being conveyed below and put into a cot in the Master's Cabin, fell into a slumber, which lasted for very many hours.

The Captain of this ship was an English Renegado, named Sparkenhoe. He had served as Midshipman and Master's Mate in a King's ship; but having been, as he conceived, unjustly Broken for hot words that passed between him and the Captain,—this took place at Gibraltar,—had deserted, and hid himself on board a Merchant Brig bound for Tangier. At last, being fond of a Roving Life (and having the misfortune to kill the Captain of the Merchant Brig in a dispute concerning some Bullocks they were shipping), he had turned Mussulman; and after living some time among the Buccaneers of the Riff, had come to Algiers, and been made Captain of a Merchantman trading to the Dardanelles, and doing a bit of Piracy when opportunity served. 'Twas full five-and-twenty years since he had Run from the King of Great Britain's service; and although his Blue Eyes and enormous Red Whiskers still gave him somewhat of a Saxon appearance, he had very nearly forgotten his Mother Tongue, and only retained English enough to enable him to mingle a few Billingsgate Oaths with his barbarous Levantine Lingo.

This fellow, whom I heartily despised, for he had kept all the Vices of his former Religion, and had acquired none of the

Virtues of his new one, was civil enough to me, and informed me that all he could do for me, in return for the Bribe he had received from his Employers, would be to deliver me to a Slave Merchant at Constantinople, who would place me out in Domestic Service where I should not be ill-treated. But he very strongly advised me to turn Turk or Renegado, as he himself was, saying, that in such a case he would land me perfectly free at the Porte, where I should doubtless find some profitable Employment. This I scornfully refused; whereupon he shrugged his Shoulders, and said that I was a Fool, but might possibly think Better of it in Time.

After three weeks' coasting among the Isles of the Grecian Archipelago, and so into the Sea of Marmora, we steered into the Dardanelles 'twixt the Castles of Europe and Asia; and the same night the Slave-Dealer comes off in a private Caique—as the Turks call their Canoes,—and the Renegado delivered me up to him. I was taken to his House at Galata, where I was kept very close for two or three weeks, and was then sold to a Merchant of Damascus in Asia, that had come to Constantinople with the Autumn Caravans, to dispose of his cargo of Silk and Attar of Roses—a very fine and subtle Perfume, one drop of which is sufficient to scent an entire House.

'Twas in the autumn of the year 1759 that I so came to Damascus, and for ten years did I remain in that city,—all the time without hearing one word from my dear Wife. Had I been in the Capital, where Foreign Ambassadors reside, I could not, as a Christian, be detained in Slavery; that being guarded against by Treaties between the Crown of Great Britain and the Sublime Porte. But in this remote part of the Empire, these and many other worse enormities were possible; and I remained as one Dead and Buried. To a few English and French Travellers passing through Damascus did I tell my piteous Tale, and entreat their help; but the account that I gave of myself was so rambling and confused, and contained, I could but confess it, many Incredible Particulars, that I could plainly see no one believed my Tale, or accounted me as aught but a half-mad Fellow that had run away for some misdeed from a Ship in port on the Coast of Syria, and was now trying to cadge Sympathy for a Pretended Grievance. At last I gave up complaining. Slowly, but surely, my memory of my former life began to Decay, and even the knowledge of mine own Language faded away, and became weaker and weaker every day. I dressed, I ate, I drank, I slept in the Eastern Fashion, and in all but religion I was a Turk.

Meanwhile I had gained in the favour of my Master. He was about mine own age when he purchased me, and we grew old Together. At first I was employed as a mere Menial, in carrying of Bales and Packages, and tending of Camels; but by degrees I was promoted to be his Warehouseman, Clerk, Cashkeeper, and at last his Partner. In that capacity he sent me to manage a large silk-plantation of his in the Lebanon; and after two years of that work I left him with a fortune of no less than five hundred Purses of Gold (about 20,000*l.* of our Money), to set up on my own account in the City of Broussa. He made no attempt (nor had he at any time done so) to combat my Religious Scruples, but counselled me to behave in all things outwardly as a Turk; and if anything was said of my being in countenance a Frank (though I was swarthy enough from my Long Journeyings), to account for it by saying that I was an Affghan born, out of India. He died very soon after I settled at Broussa, and the secret of my being a Christian died with him. It is true that, for mere Policy's sake, I did go through the Mummeries of outward Mahometans, and had my Rosary and my Prayer-carpet like other Merchants of Broussa; but I scornfully deny that I was initiated, or submitted to, any Heathenish Rites; and I am ready to maintain now, Cut, Thrust, or Backsword, that I was then as stanch and leal a Protestant as I am now.

Under the name of Gholab Hassan, of Affghanistan, and a True Believer, I prospered exceedingly, almost entirely forgetting my own country. 'Tis true I always preserved an affectionate remembrance of my dear Wife Lilias; but she seemed to me in the guise of some Departed Angel, whom I had been privileged to behold but for a Short and Transient Period. Among these Pagans, as is well known, Polygamy is permitted; but that is neither here nor there; and I was now an Old, Old Man.

'Tis ten years since, namely, A.D. 1770, that a great Insurrection against the Authority of the Porte, or rather of the Bashaw of the Province, who had been laying on the Taxes with somewhat too heavy a hand, broke out in Broussa. The infuriate Populace burnt the House of the Bashaw about his ears, plundered the Bazaar, and were proceeding to further extremities, when, a puff of my old Martial Spirit reviving within me, I collected a trusted band of Porters and Camel-drivers, rallied the Turkish Troops, who were flying in all directions, reformed them, scattered the Insurgent Mobile, and did (I promise you) speedy execution on some Scores of them. The Insurrection was very speedily subdued, and all Broussa was filled with the praises of my Valour and Discretion. The Bashaw was a poor Good-natured kind of Creature, Brave enough, but so Fat that when he mounted on Horseback they were obliged to put one of the Pillows of his Divan on the pummel of his saddle to keep his Stomach steady. An end, however, was put to the discomfort he suffered through Corpulence, by the arrival, three weeks after the suppression of the Insurrection, of a Tartar Courier, who brought with him a Bowstring and a Firman from the Grand Seignor. By means of the Bowstring, the Fat Bashaw was then and there strangled,—for they do things in a very off-hand manner in Turkey, —and when the Firman was opened by his Vizier it was found to contain, not his own nomination to the Bashawlik, which he fondly expected, but the appointment of the Merchant Gholab Hassan, that is to say,

JOHN DANGEROUS, that is to say, your Humble Servant, to the vacant Post, and commanding my immediate attendance at the Porte to receive investiture with the Three Horse-tails of Office.

I was at once saluted as Gholab Bashaw, and the next day set forth amidst great Acclamations, and in sumptuous state, for Constantinople. Arrived there, I was handsomely lodged in a Palace close to the Old Seraglio, and admitted to no less than three solemn Audiences with the Commander of the Faithful, the Caliph Al Islam, the Padishaw of Roum, the Great Turk himself.

I could not help smiling at myself, now arrayed in all the pomp and glory of an Exalted Functionary, and in the true Turkish fashion. 'Tis a custom (through Ignorance of those parts) with the Limners of Europe to portray all Osmanlis with long Beards; and, for truth, as a Merchant at Broussa, I had a great grizzled one of most Goatish appearance; but among the Bashaws and all those engaged in the

Military Service of the Grand Seignor, or holding Employments in the Seraglio, they wear only a fierce and martial pair of Whiskers. The most distinguishing sign of a true Mussulman is, after all, his Sarik or Turban, made in two parts, namely, a Bonnet, and the Linen that is wrapped round it. The former a kind of Cap, red or green, without Brims, and quilted with Cotton. About this they roll several folds of Linen Cloth; and it is a particular art to know how to give a Turban a good air; it being a trade with 'em, as the Selling of Hats is with us. The Emirs, who boast of being descended from the race of Mahomet, wear a turban all green; but that of the common Turks is red, with a white border, so distinguishing 'em from the Christians. Next I wore great long Breeches of a 'broidered stuff, and a Shirt of fine soft calico, with wide Sleeves, but no Wristbands or Collar; and over this a Cassock or Vest of fine English Cloth, reaching to the ankles, and buttoned with buttons of gold, about the bigness of a peppercorn.

This was tied with a broad Sash or Girdle, which went thrice round the waist, with the ends hanging down before, and two handsome Tassels. Over all this another Garment, richly laced, and lined with Furs of the Martin or the Badger. In my Girdle a Dagger, about the size of a case-knife, the handle curiously wrought, and adorned with Precious Stones. And as the Turkish tailors make no pockets to their vestments, Purse, Handkerchief, To-bacco-box, and things of that nature must needs be put into the Bosom, or thrust under the Girdle. Instead of Shoes, a pair of Slippers of yellow leather; which, when-ever you enter a Mosque or the presence of a Superior, you must put off on the threshold. This custom makes the soles of a Turk's feet always ready for the applica-tion of the Talack or Bastinado, from which argument neither high nor low are exempt.

Item.—-The Women here very richly dressed, but sad Gossips, and a Lazy, Lol-loping kind of creatures; which they must needs be, poor souls, seeing that they have no sort of Education, and are kept mostly in seclusion, talking of scandal, sucking of sugar-plums, showing their brave apparel to each other, and thrumming upon the Mandolin. A galloping, dreary, dull place indeed is a Turkish Harem. As to the qualities of the mind, the Turkish Women want neither Wit, Good Sense, nor Tenderness; but the constraint that is put upon 'em, and the jealous eye with which they are guarded, makes 'em go a great way in a little time, and make an ill use of the Liberty which is sometimes granted them. The old women-slaves of the Armenian and Jew Merchants, who are the confidantes of the Turkish women, enter their apartments at all hours, under the pretence of bringing them Jewels, and often favour their amours with brisk young fellows. The usual hour for intrigue is the hour of morning and evening Prayers, when the Husbands are away at the Mosques. In case of Discovery the Turks are masters of the Lives of their Wives; and if they have been convicted in form, they are sewn up in Sacks, and

thrown into the Sea.   And even if a Guilty
Woman's life is spared, she is condemned
to marry her Gallant, who is sentenced to
die, or must turn Mahometan, supposing
him to be a Christian.   The least punishment for a man who has broken the Seventh
Commandment is to ride through the streets
upon an Ass, with his face towards the Tail,
to receive a certain number of Blows upon
the Soles of his Feet, and to pay a Fine in
proportion to his Estate.

But though a duly invested Bashaw of
Three Tails, I was not fated to remain long
in that Capacity.   For once, however, my
Destiny, in subjecting me to Change, played
me a kind instead of a spiteful Turn.   Going
to visit the French Ambassador, who was
then in high favour at the Porte, I found
there, living under the protection of his
Family, a Lady, who was no other than my
dear Wife Lilias, and with her a Daughter,
called after her own name, who was now
twelve years of age.   Her History, as she
related it to me, was brief, but amazing.
Both her Father and the Cardinal died

about two years after her return from Captivity; but she found a new guardian in my old friend Captain Night, or Don Ercolo Sparafucile di San Lorenzo, the Knight of Malta, who had retired from that Island to end his days in France. She was enabled to cheer the declining years of that Gallant Gentleman, who had preserved a lively remembrance of his old *Protégé*, Jack Dangerous; and when he died, he left her the whole of his large fortune. All these years she had remained in a dreadful state of uncertainty, till, through the kind offices of the French Minister of Police, she was made acquainted with the last dying avowal of a Pirate Renegado, named Sparkenhoe, who had expired at the Galleys of Marseille, and stated that, in the year 1759, he had conveyed a refugee Christian Slave from Algiers to Constantinople, where he had been sold to a Merchant of Damascus. In the almost desperate hope of discovering some Tidings of me, my Wife and Child had journeyed to the Porte, where they were most kindly received at the French

Embassy. They had given up almost every prospect of meeting me again, when I made my sudden appearance in the strange Guise of a Turkish Bashaw.

Under ordinary Circumstances, it might have gone hard with me; for the Turks reckon it as an unpardonable crime for a Christian to assume the Mussulman Garb, and conform outwardly to that religion, without having gone through the Proper Rites. However, as I have said, the French Ambassador was just then in high favour with the Porte. He made interest with the Captain Bashaw, the Kislar Aga, and the Grand Vizier himself. The services I had rendered to the Great Turk by suppressing the Insurrection at Broussa were taken into consideration; and it was at length agreed, that if I would convey myself away privately, and take my Wife with me, no more should be said about the matter. It was given out at Broussa that I had been appointed to another and more distant Government; and he who had been Vizier to the unlucky Fat Man got his much-coveted Preferment, and, I have no doubt, was very happy in it, till the inevitable Tartar came, and he was Bowstrung, like his predecessor. So Gholab Bashaw resigned the Three Horse-tails that during so brief a period had waved at his Flagstaff, and became once more plain JOHN DANGEROUS. The Sublime Porte, however, confiscated all my Property at Broussa, including my Wives—I mean, my Women Servants.

With my Wife and Child I now returned to Europe, full of Years, and, I hope, notwithstanding some Ups and Downs, full of Honours too. We were in no hurry, however, to return to England; for I had wandered about Foreign Parts so long in Discredit, and Danger, and Distress, that I thought myself well entitled to see the world a little in Freedom and Independence, and with a Handsome competence at my Back. Therefore, as the Chevalier Captain John Dangerous,—I have dropped my Knightly rank of late years,—and furnished with all necessary passports and safe-conducts, we made our way across the Black Sea to Odessa, a mean kind of place, but rising in the way of trade; and after a most affable reception by the Russian Governor of that place, journeyed at our ease through the Tauric Chersonese, now wrested from the Tartar Khans of Simpheropol, and belonging to the Muscovites. Next, in a handsome wheeled carriage-and-four, we made for the great City of Moscow,—the old Capital of the Great Dukes of Russia,—where we abode two whole years, and went among the very best people in the place; although I had an ugly Equivoque with a young gentleman of Quality that was an officer of Dragoons, and who, I declare, stole a diamond-mounted Snuff-box of mine off my wife's Harpsichord, putting the same (the Snuff-box, I mean) into the pocket of his pantaloons. Him I was compelled to expel from my house, the Toe of my Boot aiding; and meeting him subsequently at a Coffee-house, and he not seeming sufficiently impressed with the turpitude of his Offence, but the rather inclined to regard it as a venial Prank or Whimsey, I did Batoon him within an inch of his life, and until there were more wheals on his Body than bars of silver-braid on his Jacket. This led to a serious misunderstanding between Justice and myself. I was not Imprisoned, but was summoned no less than fifty-seven times before a kind of Judge they call an Assessor, who addressed a number of interrogatories to me, which, at a moderate computation, reached, in the course of five weeks, three thousand seven hundred and nine questions. This might have gone on till Doomsday, but for the kind offices of a Muscovite friend, who hinted to me that if I discreetly slipped a Bank-bill for five hundred roubles into the hand of the Examining Judge, I should hear no more of the affair. This I did, and was soon after honourably acquitted; after which I gave the young Spark whom I had batooned his revenge, by allowing him to duff me out of a few score pieces at the game of Lansquenet. By and by, being tired of Moscow, we removed to the stately northern Capital, Petersburg, where

I had a handsome mansion on the Fontanka Canal, and was on more than one occasion admitted to an audience with the Empress of Russia, the mighty Czarina Catherine; a fine, bold, strapping woman, with a great taste for Politics, Diamonds, the Fine Arts, and affairs of Gallantry. The First time I made my obeisance to her Majesty (which was at her summer residence of Peterhoff, on the River Neva), she deigned, smiling affably, to say to me :—

"*Ah, ah! vous êtes le Sabreur anglais qui avez rossé mes gens, là-bas, à Moscou. Je voudrais que vous en fissiez autant pour mes faquins de Chevalier-Gardes à Petersbourg.*"

I was given to understand in very high quarters that I had only to ask, to receive a lucrative and honourable Appointment in the service of the Czarina,—either as a General by Land, or as an Admiral at Sea; but I was sick of fighting, and of working too; so at last, in disgust, I gave up my House, and taking shipping with my family at Cronstadt, retired to Hamburg, whence, after a brief sojourn, I travelled to France.

My sainted Wife, with whom, after our reunion, I lived most happily, died in Paris, in the year 1773; and then, feeling my Days drawing to a close, and desiring to lay my Bones in my own Country, I returned to England, after an absence of more than Thirty Years. Finding that the old Mansion that had belonged to my Grandmother was for sale by Public Auction, I purchased the Freehold, repaired and beautified it, and came to reside in it, occupying my long and happy leisure by the composition of these Memoirs. And if any one of my Readers experiences one-hundredth part the pleasure in Reading these Pages (and that I dare scarcely hope) that I have experienced in Writing them, John Dangerous will indeed be amply repaid.

THE END OF THE STRANGE ADVENTURES OF CAPTAIN DANGEROUS.

NOTE EXCULPATORY.

———

IT may be as well to state, for the benefit of sticklers for matters of fact, that, in the episode relating to Arabella Greenville, the manner of death ascribed to Lord Francis Villiers is, as Dr. Colenso would say, "unhistorical." The young nobleman in question was slain in battle; and the description of his execution at Hampton Court is one of the few instances of the Romancer's licence I have allowed myself in these volumes.

G. A. S.

R o 2 / c

CPSIA information can be obtained
at www.ICGtesting.com
Printed in the USA
BVHW081823120819
555665BV00016B/1722/P

9 780371 044636